Department of Health and Social Security

A Review of The Mental Health Act 1959

London
Her Majesty's Stationery Office

First Published 1976

ISBN 0 11 320659 3

CONTENTS

GLOSSARY OF TERMS

Admission for observation
: Compulsory admission to hospital for observation and assessment with or without other medical treatment for up to 28 days. See para 2.3

Admission for treatment
: Compulsory admission to hospital for medical treatment (including nursing, and other care or training under medical supervision) initially for up to a year. See para 1.4

Age limits
: Psychopathic and subnormal non-offender patients may not be subject to compulsory admission to hospital if aged over 21 or continue to be detained, if admitted before age 21, over the age of 25 unless likely to be dangerous if discharged.

"Approved" doctor
: Doctor approved by the Area Health Authority as having special experience in the diagnosis and treatment of mental disorder. See para 6.7

"Closed" definition
: A definition of mental disorder which would not contain the phrase "or any other disorder or disability of mind" or a similar umbrella term. See para 1.11

Compulsory admission
: Admission for observation or treatment made against the person's wishes on the basis of an application by the nearest relative or a mental welfare officer supported by one or two medical recommendations.

The Departments
: Department of Health and Social Security and Welsh Office.

Emergency admission
: Compulsory admission for observation in an emergency on the basis of one medical recommendation, for up to 72 hours. See para 2.4

Guardianship
: Compulsory control over a patient in the community which gives the guardian the same rights as a parent has over a child of under 14. See Chapter 5.

Hospital Order
: Order of the court that an offender be detained in hospital.

Informal patient
: Patient who enters and/or remains in hospital without compulsion.

Medical recommendation
: Formal written recommendation made by a doctor in support of an application for compulsory admission or hospital order.

Mental health review tribunal

Tribunal which reviews the necessity for detention of patients having, in the case of "unrestricted" patients, the right to order their discharge and, in the case of "restricted" patients, the right to advise the Home Secretary on the need for discharge. See paras 8.3–8.19

Mental Welfare Commission

See para. 8.38

Mental welfare officer

Officer appointed by the local social services department to make applications for compulsory admission and carry out certain other functions in connection with the Act. See para 6.13

Nearest relative

The closest surviving relative as defined in the Act. The Act gives the nearest relative certain rights including the right to make an application for admission and the right to order the patient's discharge. See para 6.2

Part IV

That Part of the Act which relates to compulsory powers over non-offender patients.

Part V

That Part of the Act which relates to patients involved in criminal proceedings.

Place of safety

Place, as defined, in which a person suspected of being mentally disordered can be detained, for the purpose of a medical examination and interview by the mental welfare officer, for up to 72 hours with a view to making any necessary arrangements for his treatment or care.

Regional security units

Hospital units to be set up in each health service region in England for mentally disordered patients who require more security than can be provided by local hospitals but not security of the degree provided by the Special Hospitals. (In Wales it is proposed to set up smaller secure units within existing base hospitals.)

Renewal of detention

Report made to the hospital managers by the responsible medical officer at the end of the period of detention saying that the patient still requires to be detained. See para 4.2.

Responsible medical officer

Doctor in charge of the treatment of a detained patient. He has certain statutory duties including the renewal of detention, the granting of trial leave and discretionary decisions on the withholding of his patients' mail.

"Restricted" patient

Offender patient subject to a restriction order.

Restriction order

Order imposed by the Court in addition to a hospital order which has the effect of requiring the Home Secretary's consent on all questions of leave of absence, transfer and discharge.

The Royal Commission

The Royal Commission on the Law relating to Mental Illness and Mental Deficiency 1954–1957. Report published May 1957; Command Paper 169.

Secretary of State

In this document this term has been used to mean Secretary of State for Social Services or Secretary of State for Wales. Where Secretary of State for the Home Department is intended the term "Home Secretary" has been used. It should be noted however that in the Mental Health Act—as originally enacted—the term "Secretary of State" then applied to the Home Secretary and the duties now resting upon the Secretaries of State for Social Services and for Wales were then allocated to the "Minister of Health" or the "Minister".

Special Hospitals

Hospitals provided for the treatment of detained patients who, in the opinion of the Secretary of State, require conditions of special security because of their dangerous, violent or criminal propensities.

"Treatability"

The likelihood that there will be benefit from treatment. See para 1.27.

GENERAL INTRODUCTION

1. The Mental Health Act 1959, which relates to England and Wales, is generally accepted as having been enlightened and forward-looking. In the 16 years which have passed since it came into force there have, however, been considerable changes in mental health services and practice and it seems appropriate to consider whether any amendment should be made to this important Act to bring it into line with these changes and with a view to likely developments in the future.

2. The Consultative Document is the work of an inter-departmental committee representing the Department of Health and Social Security, the Home Office, the Lord Chancellor's Department and the Welsh Office. Observers from the Scottish Home and Health Department and the Department of Health and Social Services Northern Ireland also attended although the mental health legislation for those countries is not included in the review. The Committee has had before it a number of suggestions for amendment to the Act made in recent years by various professional and other bodies and by individuals. These include the outcome of comprehensive reviews carried out by the Royal College of Psychiatrists and by MIND*. The work of the Butler Committee on Mentally Abnormal Offenders** included a review of Part V of the Act, which relates to offenders, and this Consultative Document only deals with the Committee's specific recommendations for change.

3. The Act has already been considerably amended in the course of the last decade. Parts II and III have largely been repealed by other Acts such as the Health Services and Public Health Act 1968, the Education (Handicapped Children) Act 1970, and the Nursing Homes Act 1975. No issues in relation to the remaining sections of Part II have been raised with the Departments. The remaining sections of Part III relating to residential homes for the mentally disordered are being considered by the Department of Health and Social Security as part of a wider review of the whole subject of the registration and inspection of voluntary and private homes of all types. The Personal Social Services Council also has this matter under consideration in their study of principles and practice in relation to residential care generally. Part VIII, which relates to the management of the property and affairs of patients, is the responsibility of the Lord Chancellor. He will be considering separately whether any changes are desirable in this in the light of comments received on this Consultative Document. Matters which, although they affect the mentally disordered, are the subject of legislation other than the Mental Health Act, are not included. Electoral registration is one such: the Government has already announced that it accepts in principle that mental hospital patients should be placed on the same footing as patients in other hospitals. A separate inter-departmental working group has been charged to report to the Speakers Conference on the practical issues and will shortly be producing a consultative paper.

4. This review thus mainly covers Parts I, IV and IX of the Act. It seems generally accepted that these provisions of the Act have worked well for the

---

* A Human Condition, the Mental Health Act 1959 to 1975 Vol I by Larry O. Gostin (Vol II on the law relating to mentally abnormal offenders has not yet been published).

** Report of the Committee on Mentally Abnormal Offenders: Cmnd 6244 Published October 1975.

most part but that there may now be room for improvement in certain respects. The Committee does not suggest that very fundamental change is required but that some amendment to the present Act might be beneficial to all concerned. This Document discusses the main areas in which change may be required and does so in general terms rather than by attempting a section by section appraisal of the Act or in terms of drafting specific amendments. Indeed, as is pointed out, often what is required seems to be administrative action to ensure a better understanding and application of the present legislation rather than any change to it. The arguments for and against particular changes are aired and where the arguments seem to point in a particular direction, the Document suggests what might be done; where the argument seems less weighted towards a particular conclusion, the issue is left open. It is hoped that the comments which are received in response to this Document will enable the Government to form a view as to whether the suggestions which are made for change would be broadly acceptable and what the general view is on the other issues.

5. A central question is whether and in what circumstances Society should have the right to deprive a mentally disordered person of his liberty and to impose treatment which it considers to be in his interests or those of the general public. All who have commented on the Act agree that some powers of this kind are required but there is a difference of opinion as to the extent of the powers needed. This Document takes as its basis the need to balance the rights of the patient and the needs of the public. There is a need, also, to achieve a similar balance between the interests of staff and patients and this too is discussed.

6. In considering this question it should be borne in mind that compulsory admissions to psychiatric hospitals or units are a minority of total admissions—one in eight in 1974 compared with one in five a decade earlier. Some of the issues discussed in this document are however also relevant to informal patients.

7. The arguments must of necessity be complex, involving as they do complicated systems of checks and balances. The Document is in two Parts. Part I deals with compulsory powers and Part II with the protection of patients, staff and the public. At the end of each Part is a summary of the general conclusions. It is hoped that the Document explains the problems sufficiently clearly to be readily understood by all who have an interest in these matters and wish to contribute their views. It has been sent to a wide range of bodies and organisations but should any individual wish to express a view he is welcome to do so. Comments should be sent not later than November 15 addressed to:

The Secretary
Inter-departmental Committee on the Review of the Mental Health Act 1959
Room C 421
Department of Health and Social Security
Alexander Fleming House
London SE1

PART 1

Powers for the compulsory admission and continued detention of patients in hospital and for the control of persons in the community

INTRODUCTION

The Mental Health Act 1959 includes powers for various forms of compulsory admission of patients to hospital. The arrangements for the different types of admission vary according to the type of circumstances involved although they have many common features. Chapter 1 below discusses the powers and arrangements for compulsory admission of patients for treatment; these are considered in some detail since they cover the main criteria for all forms of compulsory admission. Chapter 2 discusses powers and arrangements for compulsory admissions in cases of emergency and for observation. Chapter 3 discusses possible changes in the periods for which patients may be detained under these procedures. Chapter 4 deals with the issues of the continuation of detention and discharge. Chapter 5 discusses the powers of guardianship used for the control of persons in the community and Chapter 6 the respective roles of relatives, doctors and mental welfare officers in the arrangements for admission and discharge.

CHAPTER 1. COMPULSORY ADMISSION FOR TREATMENT

The powers

1.1 Most patients are at present compulsorily admitted to hospital for a prolonged period in one of two ways; by an application for admission for treatment under section 26 of the Act or, as a result of criminal procedings, by a hospital order made by a court under section 60.

1.2 An application for admission for treatment under section 26 may be made by the nearest relative or by a mental welfare officer; it has to be supported by two medical recommendations which agree that the patient is suffering from one or more of the four sub-categories of mental disorder mentioned in section 4(1) of the Act (mental illness, severe subnormality, subnormality or psychopathic disorder). However, if he is over the age of 21, a patient may not be compulsorily admitted to hospital only on the grounds of psychopathic disorder and/or subnormality alone. One of the medical recommendations has to be by a doctor who has been "approved" under section 28 as having had the requisite psychiatric experience and the other, if practicable, by a doctor previously acquainted with the patient. A doctor from the admitting hospital may make one of the recommendations.

1.3 A court may make a hospital order, under section 60 of the Act, in respect of an offender suffering from any of the four disorders, no matter what his age. Provided that it does not also make a restriction order under section 65, the patient is thereafter treated in the same way as a patient detained under section 26 except that his nearest relative may not order his discharge and that in the case of psychopathic and subnormal patients the special provisions relating to the expiration and renewal of the authority for detention at age 25 do not apply.

1.4 At present compulsory admission to hospital for treatment where court proceedings are not involved (ie under section 26) requires the following conditions to be satisfied:

(i) The disorder from which the patient is suffering has to be one of the following—mental illness, severe subnormality, subnormality or psychopathic disorder;

(ii) the mental disorder must be of a nature or degree which warrants detention in a hospital for medical treatment;

(iii) it has to be necessary in the interests of his own health or safety or for the protection of others that he be detained;

(iv) if the patient is suffering only from subnormality and/or psychopathic disorder he must be under 21 years of age.

1.5 The Royal College of Psychiatrists, the National Association for Mental Health (MIND) and the Committee on Mentally Abnormal Offenders (the Butler Committee) have all made suggestions which would affect these criteria. The following paragraphs discuss each of these criteria in turn; though it should be borne in mind that they are inter-related and should not be seen in isolation.

The definition and sub-categories of mental disorder

There appear to be three main alternative ways in which the definitions in the Act might be altered. The paragraphs below outline the main arguments for and against these changes. The present definitions of mental disorder and the sub-categories are set out in Appendix I.

ALTERNATIVE A: ABOLISHING THE SUB-CATEGORIES

1.6 The Royal College of Psychiatrists and others have suggested that the definition of mental disorder in section 4 should be amended on the following lines:

> "In this Act 'mental disorder' means mental illness, arrested or incomplete development of mind, and any other disorder or disability of mind however caused or manifested and 'mentally disordered' shall be construed accordingly".

Allied to this proposal is the proposition that there should be no defined sub-categories as at present. One of the reasons for this suggestion seems to be a dislike for the term "psychopathy" and a desire to avoid its use. In the above definition psychopathy would be subsumed under "any other disorder or disability of mind".

1.7 The Butler Committee have pointed out* that the present definition in section 4 with its sub-categories is the base on which the Mental Health Act rests and that changes in it would be reflected in other parts of the Act; for example adopting the Royal College proposal would widen the scope of section 60 which relates to hospital orders and would enable such orders to be made in respect of patients suffering from "other mental disorders" which are at present excluded. The Committee pointed to the difficulties which might arise if reference to psychopathic disorder were simply to be deleted and that it is one thing never to have included the term, as is the case in Scotland and Northern Ireland, but another to withdraw it after it has been in the statute for 16 years.

1.8 There would seem to be force in this argument; and if the primary aim is to abandon the use of the term "psychopathic disorder" it would seem better to do this overtly by a specific deletion or by substituting an alternative term so that all may understand the nature of the change. The question of psychopathy is discussed in more detail in paragraphs 1.20 to 1.26 below.

1.9 There is, however, another argument in favour of abolishing the sub-categories of mental disorder in favour of a wide unclassified definition of the term. Because of the imprecision of some of the sub-categories used in the Act, for example "mental illness" which is at present undefined and "whose interpretation is purely a matter of individual medical opinion", MIND have argued** that compulsory admission to hospital should be based solely on dangerousness or grave disability as shown by recent behaviour. Whether or not one accepts the need for such a narrow criterion as this, it is true that the existence of sub-categories defined as at present does not prevent difficulties arising from difference of medical opinion about the causes of certain types of

---

*Cmnd 6244: Paragraph 5.25–26
**"A Human Condition: Vol I": Page 33.

behaviour. Diagnosis is only one of the factors relevant to the need for compulsory admission; and, in practice, behaviour and the protection of the patient or others are likely to be more important factors.

1.10 The existence of sub-categories does however enable powers of compulsory admission to be limited in various respects eg at present there are age limitations in regard to psychopathic and subnormal people over the age of 21. A wider general definition would necessarily remove these limitations and broaden the powers of the Act. This may be thought to be too great a price to pay for the advantage offered.

ALTERNATIVE B: A "CLOSED" DEFINITION WITH SUB-CATEGORIES

1.11 A second alternative would be to attempt, for the purposes of compulsory admission and detention, more precise definitions of "mental disorder" and its sub-categories than those used in the 1959 Act. This would require a definition of "mental illness" which at present is undefined and the elimination of the imprecise words "any other disorder or disability of mind". This is not an easy task, indeed the Royal Commission on the Law Relating to Mental Illness and Mental Deficiency suggested that an attempt at precision was to be avoided:

> "It is far preferable that in referring to various forms of mental disorder the law should use general terms which will convey a sufficiently clear meaning to the medical profession without trying to describe medical conditions in detail in semi medical language".*

1.12 A major difficulty about attempting a precise or "closed" definition is that in seeking to ensure that it covers all the types of disorder which may warrant detention the definition may have to be drawn so widely that in practice it proves to be no narrower than the apparently vague terms "any other disorder or disability of mind". Moreover the very spelling out of detailed definitions might give an appearance of a widening of the scope and lead to an unexpected use of the powers of detention. In other words in seeking to define the scope of the powers more closely one might paradoxically unintentionally widen their effect.

1.13 Another difficulty would arise with respect to those whose main problem is a misuse of, or dependence on, alcohol or drugs. The present power compulsorily to admit for observation a person suffering from "any other disorder or disability of mind" is often usefully invoked to provide temporary protection for an alcoholic or addict who is currently a danger to himself and to enable the hospital to determine whether or not there is an underlying mental disorder. If a 'closed' definition were to omit this form of words it is not clear under which sub-category of mental disorder such people could properly be admitted compulsorily. If the term "psychopathy" were retained and "personality disorder" not substituted (see paras 1.20–1.26 below) it would not seem possible to admit them at all. If, however, the term "personality disorder" were to replace "psychopathy" other difficulties would arise since there are conflicting views of the nature of alcoholism and drug dependence, and the relationship between

---

* Report of the Royal Commission on the Law Relating to Mental Illness and Mental Deficiency 1954–1957 Cmnd 169: Paragraph 357.

these and personality disorder, when it is also present. Some doctors see drug or alcohol dependence as a form of personality disorder but this view is by no means universal. This could lead to an undesirable lack of uniformity in interpreting the law on compulsory admissions since some doctors would feel unable to admit these people at all whilst others would feel able to admit both for observation *and* for treatment.

1.14 This would still be a problem even if the view of the Butler Committee were accepted that any replacement of the term "psychopathic disorder" by "personality disorder" should be qualified to make it clear that the powers of compulsory detention should not be used on the grounds of abuse of drugs or alcohol or of sexual deviation alone. This could be achieved in respect of sexual deviation by an addition to the proviso now contained in section 4(5) of the Act concerning promiscuity or other immoral conduct; this would maintain the present position. It would be possible to add a similar proviso in respect of abuse of drugs or alcohol, either to the definition of personality disorder or, if it were desired to keep the present ability to admit for observation, to the power to admit for treatment.

1.15 On the other hand, although it is unlikely that people are now being detained under the Act who ought not to be, a decision to admit a person to hospital against his will, involving as it does his loss of liberty, is a fundamental one and there would be obvious advantage if it were possible to tighten the criteria on which such powers are based. It can be argued that using fully comprehensive and precise definitions would render decisions made under these powers more susceptible to critical examination and arbitration. This would be especially important in relation to admissions under the short term procedures where the definition now used is least precise and where there is no right of appeal to an independent tribunal. Appendix II sets out an example of what a "closed" definition might consist of.

1.16 If a "closed" definition of this sort were to be used for the purposes of compulsory admission and detention it would be necessary to include in the Act a wider definition of "mental disorder" to cover all the enabling provisions in the Mental Health Act and other National Health Service Acts which do not relate only to compulsory powers. This might well lead to confusion and must therefore be counted as a drawback to an arrangement of this kind.

ALTERNATIVE C: MODIFYING THE PRESENT SUB-CATEGORIES

1.17 A third alternative, and perhaps the best, would be to retain the present definition of mental disorder but to attempt to improve upon the definitions of some of the sub-categories involved.

"*Severe Subnormality*" *and* "*Subnormality*"

1.18 The terms "severe subnormality" and "subnormality" are no longer generally used and the Act might be amended to use the terms in current general use ie "severe mental handicap" and "mental handicap" whilst retaining the present definitions. The aim of this would not be to affect the type or range of people covered but to substitute more acceptable terms. There is a danger however that the use of the term "mental handicap" in legislation might cause confusion as it is used by some in connection with mental illnesses which have left a residual handicap eg schizophrenia. A further alternative would be to use the term "mental retardation".

1.19 The question whether mental handicap *per se* should be retained within the scope of mental health legislation at all has not been raised by the Butler Committee, the Royal College of Psychiatrists, MIND or BASW but may be thought to deserve consideration. It is however a question which raises far wider issues than are within the scope of this Chapter and a note of some of the relevant points is therefore set out separately in Appendix III. Comments would be appreciated on how the respective interests of mentally handicapped people and the general public might best be served in this connection.

"*Psychopathy*"

1.20 There has been much controversy both about the term "psychopathy" and about the practicability of providing treatment for those to whom this description is applied. The Butler Committee devoted a chapter to discussing the problem and, whilst accepting that the term was an unfortunate one which carried much stigma, saw difficulties in replacing it by the more euphemistic term "personality disorder". These difficulties lay in the potentially wide interpretation of the latter term. It clearly covers a much wider range of deviation from the "normal" than does psychopathy. The Butler Committee commented that "there may be some groups who are suffering from personality disorder or allied conditions such as sexual deviations and drug or alcohol dependence for whom it would be undesirable or unreasonable, by reason of their deviance alone, to provide for compulsory detention in hospital under civil powers"*. (See also paragraphs 1.13–1.14 above).

1.21 It is generally accepted that the term "psychopathy" has come to have unfortunate connotations and that it would be helpful if a substitute term could be found, but preferably one which does not alter the existing scope of the Act. One alternative, using the WHO definition of personality disorder as a basis, would be to use the term "severe personality disorder" and to define it as "a persistent abnormality of mind of such a kind and degree as seriously to affect the person's life or adjustment to society, and which is so marked as to render him a serious risk to himself or to others". This would, however, have a wider scope than the present definition of psychopathy especially if the present age limits were removed. (See paragraph 1.27 below.)

1.22 If the Act is still to cover psychopathy, whether under an amended definition or not, it is necessary to consider whether a proviso should be introduced into Part V of the Act of the sort which the Butler Committee suggested might be suitable for use in section 60. The form of words which the Committee suggested was:

"Save that no order shall be made under this section in the case of an offender suffering from psychopathic disorder with dangerous anti-social tendencies unless the court is satisfied:

* Cmnd 6244 paragraph 5.26.

(*a*) that a previous mental or organic illness, or an identifiable psychological or physical defect, relevant to the disorder is known or suspected; and

(*b*) there is an expectation of therapeutic benefit from hospital admission".*

1.23 This amendment to section 60 was proposed on the basis that hospitals cannot in general treat, and are not the most suitable places to contain, dangerous psychopaths with antisocial tendencies who are frequently disruptive and unco-operative. They did not think that the option of making a hospital order should be withdrawn from the court where the psychopathic offender was not dangerous and a hospital was willing to admit him. They pointed out, however, that dangerous psychopathic offenders with antisocial tendencies were usually sent to prison, and they felt that this was generally the right place for them and that the situation should receive statutory recognition. If it were later found that a sentenced psychopathic offender was after all suitable for medical treatment, and a place could be provided for him in hospital, the Committee wished it to continue to be possible to transfer him from prison to hospital under section 72 of the Act. On this basis no dangerous antisocial psychopath (other than those covered by (a) of the proviso) would, thus, be admitted to hospital without prior 'screening' within the prison system, to which the offender could be returned if his behaviour in hospital proved unacceptably disruptive or the projected treatment unavailing; it was thought that this sanction might in itself be beneficial.**

1.24 The recent White Paper *"Better Services for the Mentally Ill"* pointed out that there was "considerable uncertainty" as to how far those with personality disorders could be helped by the mental health services and that it was generally accepted that such people did not readily respond to traditional psychiatric treatment. However it also made it clear that the aim of the National Health Service should be to provide a range of facilities from the informal and open to formal security in order to deal with the varying needs of patients.*** The Butler Committee proposal would however in effect make a distinction between the NHS and the Prison Service for people suffering from the same disorder, simply on account of the degree of their dangerousness or their involvement in antisocial activity.

1.25 At first sight it might seem simpler, since it is doubtful whether effective treatment can be offered to psychopaths at the moment, to remove psychopathy from the Act altogether. However a small number of psychopathic offenders are made subject to hospital orders each year (125 in 1974) (65 of whom were admitted to Special Hospitals and 60 to local hospitals) and it would seem unfortunate to deny all possibility of hospital treatment to this group. Also, although little can be offered by hospitals at present, there may perhaps be hope of some advance in treatment methods in the future.

1.26 Thus, whilst the Committee's suggestion is a helpful one in offering legislative support to what is, in effect, the status quo it may be felt that to introduce a proviso of this kind would have little effect in practice and that it would be better to rely upon a professional judgement of what is "treatable" and to leave options open for the future. The concept of "treatability" is discussed in more detail in paragraph 1.27 below.

* Cmnd 6244 paragraph 5.40.
** Ibid: paragraph 5.41–5.42.
*** Cmnd 6233 paragraph 2.13.

Age limits and treatability

1.27 If, as in alternatives B and C above, certain categories of mental disorder were to continue to be defined in the Mental Health Act, the question would arise as to whether the age limits which at present apply to the admission and continued detention of psychopathic and subnormal patients should be retained; it would not be possible to retain them in the case of Alternative A. The application of a particular age limit is necessarily somewhat arbitrary and leads to anomalies in that similar cases may be handled differently simply because of a slight age difference. It might therefore be argued that these limits should be removed and, if possible, replaced by some alternative safeguard: for example that no application should be made for compulsory admission for treatment under section 26 without certification by the doctor that the patient is likely to benefit from treatment. This would be in line with one of the criteria which the Royal Commission recommended should be met when compulsory powers were used:

> "Good prospect of benefit to the patient from the treatment proposed—an expectation that it will either cure or alleviate his mental disorder or strengthen his ability to regulate his social behaviour in spite of the underlying disorder, or bring him substantial benefit in the form of protection from neglect or exploitation by others;"*

1.28 This recommendation was also included in the MIND Report**. There may be doubts as to how meaningful such a safeguard would be at the time of admission since judgments on the basis of prognosis are, as MIND have pointed out, unreliable. A statement of this kind would however place an extra requirement on the doctor signing the order and would necessitate a greater degree of knowledge on his part than under the present arrangements.

"Health and safety or the protection of others" or "dangerousness to self or others"

1.29 MIND have suggested*** that one of the present criteria for admission, under sections 25, 26 and 29 of the Act, namely that admission has to be in the interests of the patient's own health or safety or with a view to the protection of other persons is too broad and should be limited to relate more closely to dangerousness to self or others or to grave disablement. To limit admission by such criteria might, however, be too rigid and could prevent effective treatment being given to people who could benefit but who may be in too confused a state to realise their need. Such people would have an extra safeguard against unnecessary detention if a stronger criterion of "treatability" as in para 1.27 above was introduced.

1.30 It may, nevertheless, be argued that it is unreasonable to continue to detain a patient on the broader grounds (of health, safety or the protection of others) after he has received a period of treatment. One possibility might be to require the responsible medical officer to furnish a report on each occasion of renewal of detention that there was still a positive expectation of benefit

---

* Cmnd 169 paragraph 317.
** A Human Condition Vol. I page 144.
*** Ibid: page 33.

from further treatment; if such a statement could not be made the person should only be further detained if the doctor were to affirm that, if discharged, the patient would be dangerous to himself or to others or that he is gravely disabled. In either case the doctor would be asked to state his reasons for believing that further treatment would be beneficial or for believing the patient to be potentially dangerous or gravely disabled. These reports would need to be carefully monitored. There would, in practice, be a limit to the number of renewals of detention which could be made on the former ground but it might be unwise to impose a statutory limitation since this is a matter best left to the discretion of those who know the circumstances of the individual case, subject to monitoring and, if necessary, challenge on the reasons given. Such flexibility would seem especially important since the extent to which treatment can be expected to be of benefit will depend upon the type of case in question as well as on more individual factors. The expectation of the outcome of treatment must in general be different in the cases of the younger depressive, for example, and the elderly mentally infirm. In the former more weight would be given to the alleviation of mental disorder whereas in the latter more would be given to protection from neglect; the Royal Commission's recommendation in para 1.27 above covers both of these.

1.31 An attempt to tighten up the criteria for detention would carry the disadvantage that it could lead to some people leaving hospital who could not be detained under such strict criteria as "dangerousness to self" or "grave disablement" but who might nevertheless be expected to have some disability, possibly resulting from their illness, which whilst not "grave" nevertheless affected their ability to sustain themselves in the community, even with support.

Implications for Part V of the Act (admission of patients concerned in criminal proceedings, etc. and transfer of patients under sentence)

1.32 At present only two of the four criteria for compulsory admission to hospital for treatment discussed above apply to offenders admitted after a court has made a hospital order under section 60. They are that the mental disorder from which the offender is suffering must be one of the specified subcategories, and that it must be of a nature or degree which warrants his detention in a hospital for medical treatment. Age limits do not apply; and while the court is statutorily obliged before making a hospital order to have regard to all the circumstances, including the nature of the offence, the character and antecedents of the offender and other available methods of dealing with him, and to consider that of these a hospital order is the most suitable, there is no requirement that admission should be in the interests of the offender's health or safety or for the protection of others.

1.33 It can be argued that it is reasonable for the criteria for admission to hospital via a court to be less strict than those employed for non-offenders since in respect of any offence for which a hospital order is available to the court the offender is liable to imprisonment as an alternative disposal. As the Royal Commission said:

> "When a person has broken the criminal law he has laid himself open to the imposition of control because of behaviour which has been judged by standards which apply to all citizens. It is no longer in question whether or not he should be considered liable to control at all; the question has become whether or not one of a variety of possible forms of control provides a suitable way of treating the individual offender."*

Any change in the use of age limits for certain categories of mental disorder in relation to non-offender patients in Part IV would obviously have no effect on admissions under Part V which relates to offenders, and neither would any change in the criteria, which also applies to non-offenders, that admission must be in the interests of the patient's health or safety or for the protection of others. And while any increased emphasis on "treatability" would be relevant in so far as it might affect the court's judgement about the most suitable methods of dealing with an individual offender, it seems unlikely that this would significantly affect the number of admissions from courts.

1.34 However, any amendment to the definition of "mental disorder" or of its sub-categories contemplated in the context of Part IV admissions could have considerable implications for Part V, which would need to be carefully assessed. For example, if the words "and any other disorder or disability of mind" were to be dropped from the definition of "mental disorder" in section 4(1) of the Act there would be little point in pursuing the Butler Committee's recommendation that section 72 of the Act, which enables the Home Secretary to direct the transfer to hospital of a sentenced prisoner suffering from a mental disorder falling into one of the specified sub-categories, should be widened to include prisoners in the "other disorder" group.**

---

* Cmnd 169 paragraph 356.
** Cmnd 6244: paragraph 3.45.

CHAPTER 2. COMPULSORY ADMISSION IN AN EMERGENCY OR FOR OBSERVATION

2.1 The Act makes provision for four types of short term compulsory admissions:

(i) section 25—admission for observation (with or without other medical treatment)

(ii) section 29—emergency admission for observation

(iii) section 135—a warrant to search for and remove a patient to a "place of safety"

(iv) section 136—removal of a mentally disordered person found in a public place to a "place of safety".

The short term detention of an informal patient pending an application for admission for treatment or observation is also made possible by section 30. The five types of short term procedure are discussed below:

Sections 25 and 29

2.2 It is convenient to consider these two sections together because section 29 is often a preliminary to section 25 (although it may also be followed by discharge, informal admission or admission for treatment under section 26) and there is a feeling in some quarters that the emergency procedure is over-used.

2.3 Section 25 enables the compulsory admission to a hospital for observation of a patient whose mental disorder warrants his detention for that purpose for up to 28 days with or without other medical treatment in the interests of his own health or safety or for the protection of other people. The application for admission has to be made by the nearest relative or by a mental welfare officer and must be supported by two medical recommendations in the same way as an application for treatment under section 26 (see paragraph 1.2).

2.4 Section 29 enables an emergency application for admission for observation to be made, in a case of urgent necessity, by any relative (as defined by the Act) or a mental welfare officer on the basis of only one recommendation by any doctor. It authorises detention for only 72 hours unless a second medical recommendation, as required under section 25, is obtained within that period.

2.5 The Royal Commission made it clear that it expected the emergency procedure to be used only in exceptional circumstances:

> "It is important that the emergency procedure should not be used except in real emergencies when action to remove the patient must be taken before there is time to obtain the two medical recommendations required under the normal procedure".*

2.6 In practice section 29 has been the most used compulsory form of admission procedure and in some regions has constituted over 80 per cent of all compulsory admissions. Appendix IV sets out admissions under section 29 as a percentage of all admissions under section 25, 26 and 29 for different parts of the country between 1964 and 1973. It can be seen that for England and

* Cmnd 169: paragraph 409.

Wales as a whole admissions under section 29 have always been more than half of all these admissions; and both at the beginning and the end of the period in question they amounted to over 62 per cent of formal admissions under Part IV of the Act. The position, however, in different parts of the country varies a great deal: Oxford region had only 34 per cent of admissions under section 29 at the beginning of the period and 41 per cent in 1973, whereas in Wales section 29 admissions accounted for 88 per cent of all admissions in 1964 and for 84 per cent in 1973. Whilst most areas have remained fairly constant over the years in their use of this section an exception to this general rule is Liverpool Region which had 62 per cent of admissions in this category in 1964 but, owing to much local effort to reduce the use of section 29, had only 34 per cent of admissions in this category at the end of the period.

2.7 The high percentage of admissions under section 29 combined with the variations in its use between different areas has led to some disquiet over the years and this was expressed by the Hospital Advisory Service (now the Health Advisory Service) in its 1974 Report. Unease about this section is perhaps most marked amongst social workers. The British Association of Social Workers have suggested that section 29 should be phased out and replaced by a 24 hour psychiatric crisis intervention service whereby a team, including a social worker and a consultant psychiatrist, would attend immediately in the patient's home if necessary. The Royal College of Psychiatrists, whilst accepting the value of section 29 in certain circumstances, feel that "these advantages have led to misuse and abuse in some areas where the number of compulsory admissions under section 29 have been far in excess of those in others". The College suggests that the section be retained but that its use be the subject of continuing scrutiny by Area Health and Social Services Authorities.

2.8 As long ago as 1966, the then Ministry of Health instituted an inquiry to try and establish why this unexpected pattern of use had developed. Some interesting findings emerged which are probably still relevant today:

(i) Many medical and social work professionals were largely ignorant of the provisions of the Act and it was sometimes not recognised that section 25 should be used in all but urgent cases and that section 29 should normally be only a preliminary to either section 25 or 26.

(ii) It was suggested that because the emphasis was now on informal treatment, patients were not compulsorily detained until a situation of crisis was reached, and this in most cases involved a degree of urgency which made admission under section 29 appropriate. Community support for psychiatric patients was not sufficient to enable action to be taken to prevent an emergency.

(iii) Many professionals considered that section 29, being quicker, easier and of shorter duration was a more humane method of admitting formally than section 25. It was certainly more convenient administratively.

(iv) "Approved" doctors seemed to be rarely used. This may have been due to:

(*a*) reluctance on the part of the GP to call for a second opinion, particularly from a doctor who did not know the patient.

(*b*) individual consultants wishing to retain personal control over admissions and discouraging reference to other doctors.

(v) A hospital consultant, as alternative second opinion, might have a a number of reasons for not wishing to make a domiciliary visit; among these were time, distance, a complicated fee position, and previous knowledge of the patient which might make him unwilling to make what he considered to be an unnecessary visit.

(vi) A number of practical difficulties existed for the mental welfare officer, possibly faced with opposition from the GP and the hospital and the difficulties of getting two recommendations signed and keeping track of the patient during whatever period might elapse. There was also understandable reluctance to call a second doctor to make a visit late at night when many of these crises arose.

2.9 In general the exercise seemed to show that there were respectable reasons for the widespread use of section 29. Emergencies were much more the normal background to compulsory admissions than the Royal Commission had envisaged. In other words, to show that the section of the Act was being used more frequently than was foreseen by its framers did not necessarily mean that it was being abused. Although the main reason for the extensive use of the section appeared to be the difficulty of obtaining a second medical recommendation without undesirable delay, the overall impression was that the patient's interest was not really prejudiced by the use of this section. The Ministry, through its Principal Regional Officers, did however attempt to correct misunderstandings which gave rise to abuse and to advise on possible solutions where difficulties arose locally. The Chief Medical Officer sent a letter* to doctors in October 1966 explaining the intended use of the two sections and emphasising the importance of keeping the use of the section 29 power to a minimum. Since then the Department has received only isolated complaints about the misuse of section 29. Nevertheless the proportion of section 29 admissions has remained high.

2.10 As was indicated in the White Paper "*Better Services for the Mentally Ill*" **it is hoped that increasing use will be made of a 24 hour crisis intervention service of the sort suggested by BASW. This should eventually reduce the need for section 29 admissions but it is likely to be some time before sufficient skilled manpower and resources are available in the health and social service fields to implement this in all areas. There is likely therefore to be a continuing need for an emergency procedure on the lines of section 29; but it should be recognized that there is some danger of this procedure being used unnecessarily simply because it is administratively expedient to do so. In these circumstances, the right course seems to be to explain fully to authorities and to the professions concerned the correct usage of the section and, at the same time, to amend the forms used for admission to require a full explanation to be made by both the mental welfare officer and the doctor of their reasons for believing that emergency compulsory admission to hospital is necessary. The explanation would need to show why admission was necessary either in

---

* CMO 23/66.
** Cmnd 6233: paragraph 3.12.

the interests of the patient's own health and safety or for the protection of others, and why admission could not be delayed until a second medical recommendation was obtained. Such an explanation would obviously be meaningless unless the forms were carefully monitored and the reasons questioned where necessary. A close monitoring of the reasons given for emergency admissions might also highlight areas of difficulty for which there may be practical remedies or on which guidance might be needed.

2.11 MIND make the more fundamental suggestion that section 25 should be removed and that compulsory admission should be either a crisis intervention measure for 24 hours only or an admission for treatment for a longer period. This links with their suggestion for tightening up the criteria on which a person can be compulsorily admitted to hospital by relating this both to recent behavioural evidence that he is gravely disabled or violent and of imminent danger to himself or others, and to a prior determination that he is unwilling to enter the hospital informally and that this unwillingness is probably due to mental disorder.

2.12 There are precedents in the Mental Health Acts of Scotland and Northern Ireland for relying upon powers of emergency admission and longer periods for treatment without the availability of a 28 day observation period. However the emergency powers in these cases last for 7 days rather than for 72 hours.

2.13 The criteria for compulsory admission for treatment are discussed in paras 1.1 to 1.31 above and if, as is suggested in para 1.27, the doctor is to be asked to certify that the patient would be likely to benefit from treatment, this would restrict present powers and it would seem necessary to retain a long enough period of detention for observation and assessment in order to enable him to make a fully informed decision about both the nature and degree of the disorder and the patient's likely response to treatment. This period of observation would also be particularly important before embarking upon any of the more radical forms of psychiatric treatment. (See also paragraphs 8.28–8.29 on consent to treatment during the currency of a section 25 order).

2.14 The arguments seem therefore to point to the retention of sections 29 and 25 as they both continue to serve a useful purpose.

Section 30

2.15 This section allows the doctor in charge of an informal patient to make a report to the managers of the hospital which has the effect of authorising his detention for up to 3 days, beginning with the day the report is made, pending arrangements for compulsory admission for observation or for treatment. DHSS legal advisers interpret the section as referring only to the doctor (normally a consultant) in charge of the patient's treatment or another doctor appointed if he is sick or on official leave. Moreover the doctor must be physically present in order to examine the patient and to sign the report to the effect that he needs compulsory admission: he may not give authority over the telephone or leave a signed form in readiness for such an eventuality.

2.16 The Royal College of Psychiatrists have pointed out that difficulty has arisen over the reference to "the medical practitioner in charge of the treatment of the patient". They believe that the section is widely misunderstood and misinterpreted and that, in some hospitals, doctors other than the doctor referred to in the section sign the report. In addition they point out that the restriction causes practical difficulties, for example at night or at weekends when the consultant is not in the hospital. They therefore suggest that the section should be widened to enable a doctor "approved" under section 28 to act in the absence of the consultant in charge and to make reports under section 30. They also consider that the law should be clarified with regard to the powers to detain the patient in the interim period before the order is signed.

2.17 There is also evidence of uncertainty amongst nursing staff about their position when detaining an informal patient during the period before the doctor in charge of the patient signs the section 30 report authorising his detention—and indeed, more generally, about their position in relation to informal patients—see Chapter 9 on the protection of staff. An enquiry published in November 1975 into the circumstances leading to the death of a nurse at Tooting Bec Hospital described the uncertainty felt by nurses when dealing with disturbed informal patients and stressed that a clarification of their position would be welcome. Whilst the question of the position of staff comes more within the scope of the discussion in Chapter 9 it also has relevance to section 30 in that any delay in making a report under section 30 resulting from the fact that the doctor in charge of the patient is not available, extends the period during which the nurses have to deal with him as an informal patient. Patients too would no doubt benefit from clarification of the position.

2.18 It is therefore suggested that section 30 might be amended to enable the report to be made by an experienced Registered Mental Nurse—this would be the senior nurse on duty in the hospital with such training—and by a doctor. It may be questioned whether it would be necessary for the doctor making an order of this kind to be the doctor in charge of the patient's treatment or his deputy or, indeed, whether the signing doctor should be "approved" under section 28, since it could be argued that any of these conditions could lead to delay in obtaining the necessary report and could result in a continuation of the present difficulty. It may be argued that two signatures of this sort would provide sufficient protection for the patient against unnecessary detention. However in an important decision such as this it might be felt more appropriate to ensure that the medical recommendation is by a doctor experienced in psychiatry; this should be easier to obtain in a hospital than in other emergency situations. It might therefore be preferred that the recommendation should be by a doctor "approved" under section 28; it would be normal for the senior doctor on call to be so "approved".

2.19 If the suggestion were to be adopted it is hoped that nurses would welcome the extra responsibility. They are likely to have a closer knowledge of the individual patient and his condition than other members of staff. Such a development would also give them extra support in making the difficult decisions which confront them when the condition of an informal patient changes or deteriorates and when they feel positive action is required to prevent a potentially tragic incident either within or outside the hospital.

Sections 135 and 136

2.20 It is convenient to consider these two sections together since each gives a police officer power in certain defined circumstances to remove a person who appears to be suffering from a mental disorder to a place of safety. Section 135 provides that a Justice of the Peace may issue a warrant authorising a constable to enter any premises (if necessary by force) for the purpose of removing a mentally disordered person to a place of safety for up to 72 hours while arrangements are made for his treatment or care or his return to a hospital in which he is liable to be detained under another Part of the Act. Section 136(1) empowers a constable to remove a person from a public place to a place of safety if he appears to be suffering from mental disorder and to be in immediate need of care or control; and section 136(2) authorises such a person's detention there for up to 72 hours for the purpose of enabling him to be examined by a doctor and interviewed by a mental welfare officer and of making any necessary arrangements for his treatment or care.

2.21 Section 135 is very rarely used. The Royal College of Psychiatrists have suggested that this section needs to be more flexible in its application but the Departments have received very little comment about its use and know of no particular difficulties attributable to it.

2.22 The use of the section 136 powers is widespread, both within the Greater London area and outside it. As the Butler Committee observed*, however, the official statistics do not necessarily reflect this since, when a person is removed to a police station and admitted to hospital from there under sections 25 or 29 of the Act, the fact that section 136 powers have also been used in the removal may not always be recorded. Guidance given to the police about their powers under section 136 has been that a removal should normally be to a hospital rather than to a police station as a 'place of safety' but some police forces have had difficulty, for the reasons outlined below, in operating this guidance.

2.23 The Butler Committee recommended** that section 136 should be retained, saying that it is "both necessary and generally beneficial". They concluded that it served a useful and important service in diverting mentally disordered individuals from the criminal justice system, where this seemed appropriate to the police, and in securing rapid medical attention for them. They also cited two research studies which suggested that in most cases the people admitted to a "place of safety" by the police during the periods researched were in fact mentally disordered to the extent that their admission to hospital was justified.

2.24 MIND on the other hand have suggested*** that effect should now be given to the Royal Commission's recommendation that "the police should have power to compel [a person in a public place] to go to hospital only if his behaviour is such that he is liable to arrest under normal police powers: if he is so liable the police should be able to take him to hospital (if this seems desirable) instead of to a police station".**** MIND have also suggested***** that the power should only be exercised as a means of intervening in a crisis, that dangerous behaviour should be the basis for a decision to use the power, and that the period of detention should be reduced from 72 hours to a maximum of 24 hours. BASW

---

* Cmnd 6244: paragraph 9.4.
** Ibid: paragraph 9.7.
*** A Human Condition: Vol I page 32.
**** Cmnd 169: paragraph 412
***** A Human Condition: Vol I page 32.

have gone further by suggesting that section 136 should be phased out in favour of a psychiatric crisis intervention service and that eventually it should be removed from the statute.

2.25 The kind of situation in which section 136 is invoked is typically one in which an individual's odd behaviour is causing nuisance or offence, ie one in which, although the Act does not embody the arrestability condition proposed by the Royal Commission, he might technically be liable to arrest if only for a breach of the peace. In such a case it is desirable that the powers of removal under section 136 without arrest for an offence should be readily available to the police where there is reason to suspect that mental disorder is the cause of the behaviour.

2.26 It is felt that both sections 135 and 136 serve a useful purpose and should be retained.

2.27 However, as mentioned in paragraph 2.22, some practical difficulties have emerged in operating section 136, particularly in the Metropolitan area, in relation to the use of hospitals as "places of safety". The difficulties which have been encountered are thought to be due in part to the reluctance of some hospitals or psychiatric or accident and emergency departments to accept a person who may be violent when it has not been established that he needs hospital treatment. This is more a problem at times when the hospital is short of staff, or when it has no suitable facilities for separating him from other patients who might be harmed, or when, as in the case of some general hospitals, there may be no psychiatrist readily available. The guidance mentioned in para 2.22 is in line with a code of practice for the Metropolitan area which has been drawn up jointly by the DHSS and the Home Office and which says that normally a place of safety should be a designated hospital. The four Thames Regional Health Authorities have been asked to designate general hospitals with an accident and emergency department and 24 hour psychiatric cover as screening hospitals to take persons who are picked up more than 15 miles from the hospital normally responsible for persons from their home area. They have also been asked to identify a psychiatric hospital or unit in each Health District as responsible for patients resident in that district so as to enable the police to decide whether to take a person to the screening hospital or to the responsible hospital. Once the code of practice is fully in operation it should go some way to solving the problems.

2.28 Some social workers and others doubt whether it is right to take a person direct to a psychiatric hospital who has not first been examined by a doctor. A police station would not, however, appear to be an ideal place in which a sick person, who may be in a distressed condition, should have to remain for any appreciable time.

2.29 It may be worth considering whether it would be helpful to amend the definition of "place of safety" in the Act to something on the lines of the Scottish definition, namely:

> " "Place of safety" means a hospital as defined by this Act, or residential home for persons suffering from mental disorder or any other suitable place the occupier of which is willing temporarily to receive the patient: it shall not include a police station unless by reason of emergency there is no place as aforesaid available for receiving the patient."*

---

* Mental Health (Scotland) Act 1960: section 103(7)(b).

It is the practice of some forces to remove an apparently mentally disordered person from a public place to a hospital via a brief stay at a police station for the purpose of enabling any relevant information to be assembled and proper arrangements to be made for his conveyance to the hospital. It is not thought that any new wording should prevent this kind of arrangement continuing.

2.30 As with the other short term procedures, sections 25 and 29, it is suggested that some extra safeguard for the patient might be introduced by requiring a full explanation to be made at the time of admission as to why it was thought necessary to use compulsory powers. At present at least one police force uses a form which is handed to the hospital by the constable giving details of the circumstances surrounding his use of section 136 and any other relevant information. It might be possible to require the police in all areas to complete a similar form of which one copy might go to the hospital and the other be retained for monitoring by a senior officer.

CHAPTER 3. PERIODS OF DETENTION UNDER THE DIFFERENT TYPES OF ADMISSION PROCEDURE

Short-term Procedures

3.1 Sections 29, 135 and 136 provide for compulsory detention for a period of up to 72 hours for the purpose of obtaining more expert advice as to whether admission to a psychiatric hospital or unit is considered appropriate and necessary; section 30 enables an informal patient already in hospital to be detained for a similar period with a view to determining whether he should be formally detained.

3.2 MIND have argued that compulsory admission should be either a crisis intervention measure for 24 hours only or an admission for treatment for a longer period. Although there are arguments for reducing the periods of detention allowed by these sections this would cause considerable practical difficulties particularly in relation to weekends, holiday periods and periods of sickness and a change does not therefore seem practicable.

3.3 Section 25 allows a person to be detained for observation for a period of up to 28 days, with or without other medical treatment. The MIND suggestion in paragraph 3.2 would have the effect of abolishing section 25 admissions. The power to admit a person for a period of observation is intended to allow time for establishing whether the person is suffering from a form of mental disorder which needs to be treated and whether he is willing to undertake this treatment voluntarily. If, as is suggested in paragraph 1.27, the doctor is to be asked to certify that the patient would be likely to benefit from treatment, it would seem necessary to retain a period of detention for observation long enough to enable him to make an informed judgement and to protect the patient against longer term detention for treatment if treatment is unlikely to prove beneficial. The period of observation would be particularly important before embarking upon a longer term course of psychiatric treatment. There may be some scope for reducing the period of observation but it seems likely that a period of up to 3 weeks would be required in some cases and it thus seems sensible to leave the present period of 28 days as it stands.

3.4 These periods are of course maxima and no patient should be detained longer than is necessary to determine his needs.

3.5 It would be possible, as an alternative, to opt for an arrangement on the lines of that in the Scottish and Northern Irish Acts (see para 2.12) but, in view of the lesser safeguards provided for in an emergency admission (see para 2.4) it is doubted whether it would be generally acceptable to extend the period from 72 hours to 7 days without further safeguards being added. It should be possible to concertina the arrangements for sections 29 and 25 into a provison which enables detention in an emergency for a period of 72 hours and which can be extended for a further 4 days if a second medical recommendation is obtained but this would make it more difficult for doctors to make carefully considered judgements on treatability and might have the effect of increasing the numbers of patients who are, in the event, made the subject of the longer term powers of detention for treatment.

Longer term procedures

3.6 An admission to hospital under sections 26 or 60 lasts for up to one year in the first instance and can then be renewed for a period of one year and subsequently for periods of 2 years at a time.

3.7 The Royal College of Psychiatrists and MIND have both suggested that these periods of detention should be shortened. The Royal College in its report says:

> "It is felt that this period [2 years] is too long, tends to be at variance with the liberty of the subject and is out of line with current advances in therapy. It is recommended that sub-section 2(*b*) [of section 43] be deleted as no compulsory order should be of longer duration than 1 year except when special recommendations are made by the court."

3.8 MIND suggest that the initial detention period should be not more than 90 days and that renewal should be for not more than 120 days. Three months may however be too short a period to enable the responsible medical officer to assess the effects of the treatment which he has been providing. On the other hand any significant improvement in a patient's condition is likely to occur during the first 6 months. It is therefore suggested that the periods might be reduced by half namely to 6 months followed by 6 months followed by 1 year.

CHAPTER 4. DISCHARGE AND CONTINUED DETENTION

4.1 The discharge of a patient admitted under section 26 may be ordered by his nearest relative (as defined in the Act), the responsible medical officer, the managers of the hospital (normally the Area Health Authority), or a Mental Health Review Tribunal. However the responsible medical officer may nullify the nearest relative's discharge order by making a report to the managers of the hospital that the patient if released would be likely to act in a manner dangerous to himself or others.

4.2 If no discharge order is made during a period of detention authorised by an admission under section 26 and if the responsible medical officer considers it necessary to renew the period of detention he must submit a report to the managers of the hospital within 2 months before the expiry of the detention confirming that it is necessary in the interests of the patient's health or safety or for the protection of others that he continue to be so detained.

4.3 Some disquiet has been expressed over the fact that, whereas an application for admission for treatment must be based on two independent medical recommendations, only one report from the responsible medical officer is needed to prolong detention and this report provides complete authority for so doing. The argument for requiring a second medical recommendation to renew detention is that loss of liberty is too important a matter to rest on the shoulders of one individual. The arguments against are to an extent practical: that after a lapse of time the family practitioner will not be fully informed about the present clinical condition of his patient and may feel a natural diffidence in contesting a specialist psychiatric opinion; and that another doctor in the same hospital might be influenced by the consultant responsible for the patient, or might at least not seem to be independent; and that to obtain a second medical recommendation from a doctor with psychiatric experience but not connected with the hospital would be difficult. There is also, of course, the right to apply to a Mental Health Review Tribunal.

4.4 There is however thought to be room for some improvement in the monitoring arrangements made by health authorities to ensure that a critical examination is made of the need for the continued detention of patients and that the criteria are properly applied. Paragraph 1.30 above discusses the criteria of "health, safety or the protection of others" and "dangerousness to self or others or grave disablement" and suggests that, whilst it may be appropriate to use the former criterion at the time of admission there should come a time when, if further positive benefit from treatment cannot be expected, the latter, more strict, definition should be applied. It is not suggested however that the stricter criterion should automatically be used at, for example, the first or the second renewal of detention since the prospects of benefit from further treatment will vary from case to case but that the health authorities should institute monitoring arrangements to ensure that the stricter criterion is applied at the right time.

CHAPTER 5. COMPULSORY POWERS IN THE COMMUNITY (GUARDIANSHIP)

5.1 Under the Mental Health Act guardianship gives to the guardian powers equivalent to those a parent has over a child of under 14 years. Applications for powers of guardianship can be made in respect of a person of any age on the grounds that he is suffering from mental illness or severe mental subnormality or of under the age of 21 if he is suffering from psychopathy and subnormality, provided always that it is in the interests of the person concerned or for the protection of others. Powers last initially for 1 year, renewals being for one year in the first instance and thereafter at 2 yearly intervals. Those suffering from psychopathy and subnormality cease to be subject to guardianship at the age of 25. All persons subject to guardianship have the right of application to the Mental Health Review Tribunal.

5.2 Statistics show that the number of guardianship cases involving the mentally handicapped has fallen considerably and steadily since the year 1959. For the mentally ill the figures have always been very low without any particular trend upwards or downwards. (See Appendix V) The figures show marked regional variations. An analysis of the 1973 totals shows that 24 out of 46 old style county councils had guardianship cases and, of those, 2 councils accounted for 28 cases out of a total of 95. Of the 79 county boroughs, 25 had cases but 3 of them accounted for 23 cases out of a total of 70. Out of 33 new London Boroughs only 7 had cases and one of these accounted for 13 out of a total of 26 cases.

5.3 Under the present legislation guardianship provides the only effective form of control for those mentally disordered adults in the community for whom some form of compulsory powers are required over a substantial period of time; the vast majority, however, receive care or treatment on a voluntary basis.

5.4 The working parties of the Royal College of Psychiatrists and MIND, and also the Butler Committee, all felt that more use could be made of guardianship as an alternative to hospital treatment; but they have not suggested any change in the law. The Butler Committee recommended that there should be closer liaison between the courts and the Social Services Departments of local authorities.

5.5 Although at first sight the guardianship powers seem to offer a useful half-way measure between detention in hospital and complete freedom in the community, it is difficult to endorse these recommendations without reservation in the face of the wide variation in patterns of usage which is evident from the statistics available. Before agreeing that greater use should be made of guardianship, therefore, it is suggested that further information about the reasons for these differences should be obtained.

5.6 If age limits were removed from the provisions relating to compulsory admission to hospital for treatment (see paragraph 1.27 above) consideration would need to be given to whether the same would need to be done in the case of guardianship, especially since the alternative criterion of treatability could not be applied. Any shortening of the periods of detention in hospital would presumably need to be accompanied by an equivalent reduction of the guardianship periods.

CHAPTER 6. THE ROLES OF RELATIVES, MENTAL WELFARE OFFICERS AND "APPROVED" DOCTORS IN ADMISSION AND DISCHARGE PROCEDURES

6.1 References have been made at various points in the previous paragraphs to the parts played by relatives, mental welfare officers and doctors "approved" under section 28 of the Act in the admission and discharge procedures. They all play key roles.

Role of relatives

6.2 The nearest relative (as defined by section 49(1)) of a patient liable to be compulsorily admitted to hospital under the Mental Health Act has, if he chooses to make use of the powers given to him by the Act, an important function in admission and discharge procedures. An application for emergency admission under section 29 may be made by *any* relative (as defined) or by a mental welfare officer. In the case of admission under section 25 or section 26 it is only the *nearest* relative or a mental welfare officer who can apply. The discharge of a patient admitted for treatment under section 26 may be ordered by the nearest relative who, however, must give 72 hours written notice of his intention. If within that period the responsible medical officer reports to the hospital managers, certifying that in his opinion the patient if released would be likely to be dangerous to himself or others, the order for discharge is ineffective; but the nearest relative must be informed and may within 28 days apply to a Mental Health Review Tribunal in respect of the patient. Apart from these powers, the nearest relative has the right, if an application for admission for treatment of the patient is proposed by a mental welfare officer, to notify that officer or his employing authority that he objects to such an application being made and his objection is a bar to such an application. If this power to object is used unreasonably by the nearest relative however, an application may be made to the county court for the appointment of an "acting" nearest relative (usually the local authority) in his stead under section 52.

6.3 The suggestion is made in the MIND report* that relatives should cease to be involved in the admission or discharge of compulsorily detained patients. The report says that the relative may, because of his emotional involvement, be unable to see what is best for the patient and may, indeed, be a contributing factor to his mental disorder. The report goes on to say that the fact that it is his application which places the patient in hospital, may be the cause of a long-lasting breach in their relationship. The nearest relative's power to order discharge has similar disadvantages, in that the patient may blame him for not ordering his discharge.

6.4 There are arguments both for and against continuing the nearest relative's involvement at the admission and discharge stages and that of other relatives in emergency applications for admission. The powers are permissive and it is therefore possible for the relative to choose how active a part to play. Although most applications for admission seem to be made by mental welfare officers some close relatives may prefer to feel that they are in control of the situation. The relative may have more insight into the patient's likely behaviour and will

---

* A Human Condition: Vol I pages 43 and 44.

almost certainly be able to judge better than anyone else whether he is unable to cope with the patient. It is at present the widely held view that, the greater the involvement of the patient's family, the better the chances of rehabilitation in the broad sense.

6.5 The other view is that it is unrealistic to expect the nearest relative, or indeed any relative, always to have the patient's best interests at heart or to know how to achieve what is best for him. His involvement leaves the way open to misuse, whether intentional or not. The emergency procedure under section 29, as has already been pointed out, has been used much more frequently than was expected and there is reason to believe that the vast majority of emergency admissions take place at night or during the weekends when medical or social work staff are difficult to contact. There is considerable pressure on those involved in a crisis with a mentally disordered person at night to find a solution quickly and with a minimum of inconvenience. The person likely to be contacted is the family practitioner who may not have had specialised post-graduate training in psychiatry. He will wish to place the patient in the hands of those who can deal with the crisis more effectively. The relative will probably feel the same and may be fairly easily persuaded to make an application for admission. He will be unlikely to insist on a second medical opinion before doing so. Apart from the fact that the emergency provisions are used more often than was contemplated by the framers of the Act, there is the additional factor that there has been considerable change in family doctor services since the passing of the Act. Because of the increasing use of group practices and agency services it is now less realistic to rely upon the family practitioner who attends a night call being the particular doctor who has a knowledge of the patient and his history. The decision to make an application under section 29 might thus depend upon the recommendation of a doctor with little personal knowledge of the patient or of mental disorder and of a relative who is certainly not impartial, is not necessarily motivated to act in the best interests of the patient and may be ill-equipped to make a proper judgement about the need for admission to hospital.

6.6 If it were decided that the nearest relative should retain his right to make an application for admission of a patient, it seems clear that he should also have the right to order his discharge. The converse is not necessarily true: it may be desirable to leave him the right to order discharge as an additional safeguard even if it is decided to discontinue his right to apply for admission. Comments are invited on whether it is thought that relatives should continue to have the right to apply for admission and order discharge and on what the role of the nearest relative in discharge procedures should be.

Doctors "approved" under section 28

6.7 Section 28 of the Act sets out which doctors may give the medical recommendations required in conjunction with an application for admission to hospital under sections 25, 26 and 29. They will normally be a family practitioner who knows the patient and a doctor approved under section 28(2) as having special experience in the diagnosis or treatment of mental disorder. Since the National Health Service Reorganisation Act 1973 the responsibility for approving doctors for this purpose rests with the Area Health Authority with the advice of a panel of psychiatrists.

6.8 Three main practical difficulties have arisen over the operation of this section:

(i) there are not enough section 28 "approved" doctors;

(ii) some of them are insufficiently qualified;

(iii) sub-section 3 of section 28, which requires that only one of the medical recommendations should be made by a doctor employed by the receiving hospital, is causing problems.

These difficulties are discussed in the following paragraphs.

6.9 The shortage of section 28 "approved" doctors has concerned mental welfare officers for many years and is one of the factors responsible for the large number of admissions under section 29. In 1974, at the time of the reorganisation of the Health Service, Area Health Authorities were asked to "encourage an adequate number of suitable medical practitioners"* to apply for approval under section 28 and to ensure that at least 2 doctors on the staff of every hospital which received detained patients were so approved.

6.10 The question of qualifications has now, as the Royal College point out, been resolved by referral to the Court of Electors which is a committee of the Royal College of Psychiatrists whose function is to approve training posts and the qualifications required for membership of the Royal College. The Court of Electors has advised that suitable qualifications and experience are a Diploma in Psychological Medicine (DPM), eligibility for a DPM and other equivalent psychiatric experience or training. There is, however, some feeling that the qualifications should be higher than these and that only doctors at present practising psychiatry for at least a few sessions a week should be eligible to be approved under section 28. However, the higher the qualifications demanded the more acute the shortage of "approved" doctors is liable to become.

6.11 Sub-sections 3 and 4(e) of section 28 provide for only one of the medical recommendations to be made by a doctor on the staff of the receiving hospital. Community medicine has recently been developing in such a way as to produce greater integration with the hospital service and the result is that many family practitioners are employed on a part-time basis as clinical assistants. If such a doctor signs a medical recommendation certifying that one of his patients requires to be formally admitted to hospital under the Mental Health Act and the hospital concerned is the one at which he carries out his sessions as a clinical assistant, even if his work is in a totally unrelated field such as gynæcology the second medical recommendation cannot be signed by a psychiatrist from the same hospital. This practical difficulty is likely to continue and it, of course, aggravates the situation if the limited number of section 28 "approved" doctors cannot be made use of. It is suggested that the legislation should be amended to enable both medical recommendations to be made by doctors employed by the receiving hospital, providing one of the doctors works most of his sessions elsewhere.

6.12 The other problems appear to be more a matter for guidance than new legislation.

---

* HSC(IS)18 and WHSC(IS)19.

Role of the Mental Welfare Officer

6.13 The mental welfare officer replaced the "duly authorised officer" when the Mental Health Act was introduced in 1959. He has the important function of making the application for the admission of a mentally disordered person to hospital if the nearest relative does not wish to do so himself or if there is no nearest relative. Section 54 states, rather imprecisely, what is required of him:

> "It shall be the duty of a mental welfare officer to make application for admission to hospital . . . . where he is satisfied, having regard to any wishes expressed by relatives of the patient or any other relevant circumstances, that such an application ought to be made and is of the opinion that it is necessary or proper for the application to be made by him."

6.14 With the transfer of hospital social workers to local authorities following the reorganisation of the National Health Service, some authorities authorised these social workers to undertake the duties of mental welfare officers. As the question was raised whether an assesment carried out by such a mental welfare officer could be seen as being independent in relation to patients admitted to their own hospital, other authorities appointed only social workers with no such connection with the psychiatric services. Some authorities have appointed all their social workers to undertake statutory duties. The Hospital Advisory Service Report for 1974 points out that this can result in social workers who hold no recognised professional qualifications being appointed to act as mental welfare officers. The use of non-specialist social workers seems to have had two effects: firstly to vary the quality of service available to the patient and the protection afforded to him by the mental welfare officer, and secondly to question the level of expertise required to be a mental welfare officer and consequently the kinds of judgements he should be making. The non-specialist social worker may not feel he has sufficient status to disagree if the doctor considers that compulsory admission is necessary. He may therefore yield to pressure exerted by the doctor and sign the application even if it is against his better judgement. The MIND Report stresses the important role of the mental welfare officer in protecting the patient against unwarranted compulsory admission to hospital. But its suggestion that the mental welfare officer should be required by law to examine the patient independently of the doctor and to make a statement to the effect that he has done so and that in his opinion the person requires to be compulsorily admitted to hospital would not solve the fundamental problem.

6.15 It seems that at present the role of the mental welfare officer in compulsory admission may be viewed in three different ways: firstly that of a worker representing the relative who does not wish to be instrumental in the detention of the patient; secondly that of a professional social worker judging the need for compulsory admission on the basis of social work expertise with medical advice; or thirdly that of a professional social worker with specialist mental health training and experience which enables him to make an informed decision as to whether or not he should make the application. The different levels of expectation inherent in these three interpretations of the mental welfare officer role have led to some confusion.

6.16 They can, however, be seen as different levels of expectation rather than as different concepts of function. There has been much progress in the development of social work and in professional training since the passing of the 1959 Act. In 1959 whilst the newly created mental welfare officer had experience in the psychiatric field only a few had specific training as such. At that time it was therefore only reasonable to expect the first level of involvement as a general rule (although individuals might function at a considerably higher level). With the development of the social work profession and the increased numbers of workers who have received training it can now be generally expected that the second level of involvement should apply. In Chapter 9 of the recent White Paper, *"Better Services for the Mentally Ill"* recent developments in providing specialist post-basic training for social workers in the mental health field were outlined and the need for training to be given to social workers assigned to statutory duties in relation to the Mental Health Act was stressed. The White Paper said that in-service training should, as a minimum, be available. The third level of expectation may therefore be considered as the one which should be worked towards as this training develops. Whilst the three levels may thus be taken as broadly indicative of the past, present and future situations there have, so far, always been variations in the level of social work expertise that may be brought to bear in any particular situation. As has been pointed out there have been, from the time of the passing of the Act, individuals who had more expertise than could generally be expected. Similarly there are today social workers who, because of inexperience or lack of training, are able to operate only at the level lower than that which is now generally expected. With time and further developments in training it is hoped that these differences will be evened out and that the more expert level of social work involved in these crucial decisions will become the rule.

6.17 No change of law seems to be needed but there may be a need for some code of practice in this field on formal admission procedures. The Departments propose to consult with the professions about this and also about problems which arise from time to time on the practical operation of the sections of the Act. Some of these are getting a hospital place for the patient, getting hold of the doctor, escorting the patient to hospital and the practical operation of the provisions of section 136.

CHAPTER 7. SUMMARY AND CONCLUSIONS TO PART 1

7.1 The definitions of mental disorder and its sub-categories are discussed. There are advantages and disadvantages both in omitting the sub-categories (paras 1.6—1.10) or attempting a "closed" definition with precise definitions of sub-categories (paras 1.11—1.16). There would seem most advantage in retaining the existing form of definitions but possibly with an attempt at improving the definitions of some of the sub-categories (paras 1.17—1.26). The question of whether mental subnormality should be removed from the Act altogether is referred to (para 1.19). A note of some of the relevant points is at Appendix III.

7.2 There seems little case for retaining the age limits which at present apply to the admission of patients suffering from psychopathy and mental subnormality but if these were to be removed there is a case for introducing a stronger criterion of "treatability" to apply to all the sub-categories of mental disorder. (Paras 1.27—1.28).

7.3 The suggestion that the criterion of compulsory detention needing to be in the interests of the "health, safety or the protection of others" should be replaced by the narrower criterion of "dangerousness or grave disablement" is discussed (paras 1.29—1.31). It is felt that the broader criterion should be retained at the time of admission but that the more strict criterion should be applied upon a renewal of detention if there is not likely to be positive benefit from further treatment.

7.4 Consideration would need to be given to the implications for Part V of any changes in Part IV. (Paras 1.32—1.34).

7.5 The use of sections 25 and 29 is discussed in the light of criticisms about the extent of the use of emergency powers and of the wide variation in the use in different parts of the country. Whilst it is felt that there is a need to retain the powers in both sections there may be scope for improving, by administrative action, the use that is made of them. Such action would include the amendment of the forms of application and the monitoring of the reasons given for their use. (Paras 2.1–2.14.)

7.6 It is argued that the powers in section 30 should be retained but that there would be advantage in altering the arrangements to reduce the difficulties which arise over delay in determining the status of patients. It is suggested that the necessary reports could be made by a senior nurse and by a doctor. It is open to debate whether or not the doctor need be "approved" under section 28. (Paras 2.15–2.19.)

7.7 Section 135 is rarely used but no particular difficulties are attributed to it and it is suggested that it should be retained. (Paras 2.20–2.21.)

7.8 There have been some problems over the use of section 136, particularly in relation to the use of hospitals as "places of safety" in the Metropolitan area. It is thought that the section should be retained and that the problems should be eased once a Code of Practice which has been drawn up for the Metropolitan area is fully in operation. However it is suggested that there might be some merit in amending the Act to make it clear that a hospital should normally be the "place of safety" and that a police station should be used only in the last resort. The use of the powers in the section should be monitored. (Paras 2.22–2.30.)

7.9 Practical considerations seem to preclude reducing the periods of possible detention under the short-term procedures from the present periods of 72 hours or 28 days. (Paras 3.1–3.5.)

7.10 However it is suggested that the periods of possible detention for treatment should be reduced by half from the present periods of one year followed by one year and subsequently 2 years at a time to 6 months, 6 months and subsequently periods of 1 year. (Paras 3.6–3.8.)

7.11 It is not thought that a requirement should be introduced for a second opinion to be sought when renewing the authority to detain a patient; but it is suggested that after an initial period of treatment a tighter criterion for continued detention should be introduced and that renewals of detention should be monitored. (Paras 4.1–4.4.)

7.12 The use of the powers of guardianship is discussed in the light of recommendations that they should be used more often. In view of the wide variation in the use of these powers in different parts of the country it is felt that further information should be sought. (Paras 5.1–5.6.)

7.13 The roles of relatives in the admission and discharge procedures are considered and views are sought on the extent to which they should continue to be involved in these. (Paras 6.1–6.6.)

7.14 The problems relating to the use of doctors "approved" under section 28 are discussed and are felt to be, in the main, matters for administrative action. However it is suggested that, in the light of recent developments in community medicine, the legislation might be amended to enable both medical recommendations to be made by doctors employed by the receiving hospital providing one of the doctors works most of his sessions elsewhere. (Paras 6.7–6.12.)

7.15 There is some confusion about the role of the mental welfare officer in the admission procedures but it is argued that this is due largely to changes within the social work field since the passing of the 1959 Act and that no legislative change is required. (Paras 6.13–6.17.)

PART II

Protection of the Patient, Staff and Public

INTRODUCTION

In its Report in 1957 on which the present Mental Health Act was based the Royal Commission on the Law Relating to Mental Illness and Mental Deficiency said:

> "The proper treatment of people suffering from disorders of the mind, and any restrictions on the liberty of individual citizens which this may involve, are matters of public interest which may at any time become of immediate personal importance to anyone living in this country."*

The Commission went on to argue:

> "The administrative methods by which proper standards of care are to be maintained should not now be linked to the procedures prescribed for detained patients. Helpless patients should receive proper care whether or not they are, for other reasons, subject to powers of detention or control. Compulsory powers should then be used only when they are positively necessary in order to override the wishes of the patient or his relatives for the patient's own welfare or for the protection of others."**

Whilst the philosophy behind these statements remains valid today, it seems appropriate to examine, in the light of the practical experience gained over the past 16 years, the working of the arrangements which the Mental Health Act 1959 introduced to put this philosophy into effect.

The central concept of the Act is that a patient should only be treated under compulsory powers if it is necessary in the interests of his own health or safety or for the protection of others. Its main concern is with the balance between the protection of the public and the patient and it also recognises the fact that, in consequence of their actions in operating its provisions, those responsible may require legal protection.

The question of compulsory admission and detention has been discussed in Part I. This part of the Document relates to those aspects concerned with the protection of patients, staff and the public. Chapter 8 discusses the protection of the patient, including the functions of MHRTs; Chapter 9, arrangements for the protection of staff; and Chapter 10, the protection of the public.

---

* Cmnd 169: paragraph 63.
** Ibid: paragraph 135.

CHAPTER 8. PROTECTION OF THE PATIENT

Developments since the 1959 Act

8.1 The Royal Commission felt that the Board of Control's responsibility for matters affecting individual patients and the procedures applied to them, especially procedures which authorise detention, would be better taken on by a new system of Mental Health Review Tribunals and that the inspecting functions of the Board could be better carried out by informal means, for example, by correspondence and personal discussions rather than by a formal inspection procedure. They left the question open however as to whether regular inspections of the hospitals should be carried out in addition to other methods of consultation. The Commission said:

> "In our view it is preferable that enquiries should be held by or on behalf of those authorities who have power to take disciplinary action should the complaint be substantiated, or to exert other forms of pressure to prevent a recurrence".*

The management of the property and affairs of patients were not within the terms of reference of the Royal Commission and Part VIII of the Act thus made little change to the existing laws. The Court of Protection and the Lord Chancellor's Visitors continue to carry out their functions in this area.

8.2 Since the passing of the Act in 1959 which brought these recommendations into force there have been several major enquiries into the arrangements for care of patients in individual hospitals. Partly as a result of these enquiries and partly because of a more general recognition of the need for more effective mechanisms for examining the services and for investigating complaints, a number of developments have taken place:

(i) an independent advisory service, the Hospital Advisory Service** was established in 1969 to advise the Secretary of State on standards of care and management practices in individual hospitals. Whilst not a means of formal inspection on the lines of the old Board of Control, the HAS does fulfil, in a more formal way than was envisaged by the Royal Commission, some of the functions which the Commission felt more appropriate to the central Department and health authorities. Its functions have recently been extended, particularly in relation to follow-up of its recommendations and to carrying out its work in co-operation with the Social Work Service.

(ii) Health Service and Local Government Commissioners have been appointed with powers to investigate individual complaints referred to them. If a patient is unable to act for himself a complaint may be made to the Health Service Commissioner on his behalf by a person or organisation suitable to represent him. The Commissioner can investigate a complaint which has not first been brought to the authority's attention if the patient cannot act for himself and a member of the hospital staff submits the complaint for him, if the Commissioner feels that the particular circumstances warrant this.

---

* Cmnd 169: paragraph 744.
** Now the Health Advisory Service.

(iii) Community Health Councils have been established with functions which include visiting health establishments, acting as "patient's friend" and reporting to the public on their activities. As far as complaints are concerned their function is spelt out in Appendix 5 to HRC(74)4 (in Wales, Appendix 2 to WHRC(74)3) as:

"... without pre-judging the merits of individual complaints or seeking out the facts, to give advice, on request, on how and where to lodge a complaint and to act as a "patient's friend" when needed. A CHC will also wish to bring any potential general causes of local complaint to the notice of the AHA".

CHCs have no statutory function to represent the interests of the community in local authority services.

(iv) A National Development Group for the Mentally Handicapped composed of independent professional experts has been established to advise the Secretary of State for Social Services and play an active part in the development both of Departmental policy and the strategy for its implementation. A Mental Handicap Development Team has also been set up to work closely with the NDG. It includes people with specialist knowledge and practical experience and its function in England is to provide advice and information to health and local authorities at field level, particularly on the joint planning of services, and to encourage good practice. It will visit hospitals and residential accommodation for the mentally handicapped but will not investigate responsibility for the care and treatment of individual patients or residents.

(v) Following the recommendations made by the Davies Committee in its Report on Hospital Complaints Procedures, it has been accepted that there should be a uniform written code for the handling of complaints in all establishments and the control of health authorities rather than different arrangements for different types of hospitals. A draft code of practice for health authorities and their staff, and an accompanying draft guidance circular, have been issued for wide consultations. The proposed new complaints procedure envisaged that health authorities would investigate and reply to all complaints including those involving clinical judgment. The Davies Committee also recommended that an investigating panel should be established in each health service region to investigate complaints at present outside the jurisdiction of the Health Service Commissioners. Most complaints of this kind involve the exercise of clinical judgement. This proposal has been criticised on a number of grounds. A particular aspect of concern is the danger of overlapping of functions between the panels and the Health Service Commissioners and consequent confusion to the public. The Select Committee on the Parliamentary Commission for Administration has been asked to undertake a review of the present jurisdiction of the Health Service Commissioners for England, Wales and Scotland in respect to hospital services having regard to the recommendations of the Davies Committee about investigating panels. A key issue it will be considering will be whether there should be machinery for an independent review of complaints involving clinical judgement.

Mental Health Review Tribunals

8.3 Mental Health Review Tribunals (MHRTs), recommended by the Royal Commission, were introduced in the 1959 Act. Their role is to prevent unnecessary continued detention of patients in hospital or under guardianship. Various suggestions have been made about their functions, their powers and their constitution and these are discussed below.

8.4 The Royal College of Psychiatrists have suggested that the work now being done by MHRTs should be undertaken by mental welfare commissions on the lines of the Mental Welfare Commission in Scotland. The suggestion that mental welfare commissions might also be introduced in England and Wales is discussed in paragraphs 8.38–8.42 but insofar as the suggestion relates to the discharge function of MHRTs, it should be pointed out that, although the Scottish Commission has power to discharge an individual patient it usually does so as part of its general duty to protect the interests of patients and not as part of a review for this specific purpose. The more direct counterpart in Scotland is the Sheriff to whom there is a statutory right of appeal at stated intervals. Thus, while the introduction of commissions on the Scottish lines might provide a useful supplement to the powers of the Tribunals, it is not thought that they would be fully adequate in themselves in this respect in England and Wales.

8.5 The MIND Report makes a number of suggestions* about Mental Health Review Tribunals in relation to their functions, powers and procedures. Much space is devoted in the Report to the procedures of Tribunals and suggestions are made on such issues as representation at a Tribunal, whether hearings should be in public or in private, whether they should be formal or informal and whether decisions should be made public. It is not proposed that these detailed procedural issues should be dealt with in this Consultative Document but, since a review of Tribunal procedures would now seem helpful, it is proposed that a separate review should be conducted by the Lord Chancellor's Department, DHSS, and Welsh Office in which the Council on Tribunals and the Mental Health Review Tribunal Chairmen will be invited to participate. The procedures are set out in the Mental Health Review Tribunal Rules 1960 and changes would not require amendment of the Mental Health Act.

8.6 MIND make two alternative suggestions for changes in the operation of MHRTs. The first is a very fundamental one, namely that the present machinery should be replaced by alternative arrangements by which all cases of compulsory admissions would be required to be reviewed within 5–10 days of admission and formal applications would have to be made to Tribunals for continued detention. MIND appreciate that this may not be practicable and have suggested as an alternative that automatic periodic reviews should be introduced for patients who have not been seen by a Tribunal on the grounds that some patients lack the initiative to ask for their cases to be reviewed. This seems an acceptable answer to the problem of the patient who lacks the initiative to apply for a hearing.

---

* A Human Condition: Vol I pages 56–99.

8.7 The idea of automatic review for those who have not exercised their right to apply to a Tribunal has obvious attractions. If the present periods of detention were halved, some unrestricted patients would be likely to apply to a Tribunal for a hearing more often; but this alone would not be likely to affect those patients who now do not exercise their rights. Automatic reviews would be one way of ensuring that everyone's case received independent scrutiny. On the other hand, there may be a danger that if automatic hearings were too frequent they might degenerate into a mere formality with the Tribunal failing to treat each case with sufficient care. The Royal Commission were alive to this danger and felt that the members of Tribunals should be people who were called on to consider cases comparatively rarely, and that changes in membership should be made from time to time. (However, it seems that this may have been at least counter-balanced by lack of experience, and that some reconsideration of this policy may be in order). If reviews were too frequent and patients felt that hearings were not dealt with thoroughly, this might have a bad effect on morale. Another argument which might be raised against automatic reviews is that the knowledge that a Tribunal would be considering their patients' cases in due course might have the effect of discouraging some consultants from reviewing them themselves. On the other hand some consultants might take extra care to review cases before a Tribunal hearing fell due. The arguments appear to point to there being a need for automatic reviews, but at well spaced intervals.

8.8 If automatic reviews were to be introduced it might be thought to be simpler both for patients to understand and to administer without error if *all* detained patients were to be given automatic reviews at fixed periods of time rather than such reviews being limited to those who have not previously exercised their right to apply. It would in this case be necessary to ensure that a patient who had previously exercised this right did not have two hearings too close together and to provide for a minimum of perhaps six months between hearings.

8.9 There is also an argument for automatic review of the cases of "restricted" patients. Such patients are in a special position since they have no right of direct application to a Tribunal and since there is no need for the authority for their detention to be renewed. The Home Secretary is, however, required by the Act to refer to a Tribunal for advice on the case of a "restricted" patient, after receiving a request from him for this to be done, and this is an important means by which the patient can have reviewed the need for his continued detention or the maintenance of the restriction. "Restricted" patients can request a reference after one year and then once every two years. Even if it were made possible for them to request a reference more frequently, there would be some "restricted" patients who would still fail to exercise their rights to do so. The gap could be filled by an additional procedure under which the Home Secretary would initiate an automatic review by a reference to a Tribunal for advice. There would also in this connection appear to be merit in the Butler Committee recommendation that existing good practice should be formalised by requiring the responsible medical officer to make annual reports on his "restricted" patients to the Home Secretary.

8.10 At the time of the introduction of the 1959 Act, it was not clear how many cases might be heard by Tribunals. Experience has shown that these have been far less than the 7–8000 cases expected. So far the largest number has been 1,515 in England and Wales (in 1967) and since then the numbers have declined to 843 in 1971. The original over-estimate led to far too many members being appointed and many did little or no work during the period of their appointment. Because replacements have not been made following resignations or deaths, the panels of members are now much reduced and there are at present about 580 Tribunal members in England and Wales—(this figure comprises 100 or so legal members, 12 of whom have been appointed as chairmen, about 215 medical members and about 200 lay members). Some members have very little experience during their period of appointment and it is thought that an increase in the number of cases would not present difficulty so far as lay and legal members are concerned. There is less certainty as to how much additional work could be taken on by the present medical members or whether sufficient experienced new medical members would be available to deal with a substantial increase. But some increase should be possible, perhaps a doubling of the present workload.

8.11 It is estimated that at present some 3,500 people are eligible each year to ask for a Tribunal hearing although fewer than 1,000 exercise this right. If the periods of detention were halved except in section 65 restriction order cases, some 6,000 patients a year would be eligible to ask for a hearing. While it seems that some increase in workload can be accepted, it is unlikely that automatic reviews could be introduced for each period of continued detention or indeed that this would be advisable in the light of the arguments set out above. A doubling of the present workload would enable automatic reviews to be introduced on a modest scale, for example either at the end of the first year and the fifth year of detention or at the end of the first six months and the fourth year of detention. For "restricted" patients automatic review as early as the first year would not seem appropriate and the automatic review might be limited to the fourth or fifth year. Automatic reviews at shorter periods could only be achieved if the workload were correspondingly increased and this may not be practicable. Particular problems would arise in those regions in which a Special Hospital is situated since these produce a large number of cases for review and special arrangements might have to be made for these regions. Comments would be welcomed, in particular from MHRT Chairmen and members, on the feasibility of increasing their workload and by how much it would be possible to do so.

8.12 Another question on which the Butler Committee, the Royal College of Psychiatrists, MIND and BASW have all commented is the extent and range of powers of Tribunals. At the moment Tribunals may direct the discharge of any patient whose case they are hearing (except one subject to restrictions) and must direct his discharge if they are satisfied (i) that he is not suffering from one of the four categories of mental disorder specified in the Act or (ii) that it is not necessary in the interests of his health or safety or for the protection of others that he should continue to be detained or (iii) in the case of a patient reported as likely to act in a manner dangerous to himself or to others, that this is no longer the case. In the light of a small number of cases of ex-patients discharged by Tribunals later committing serious offences, it has been suggested by some that MHRTs should not have the power to discharge patients against the advice of the responsible medical officer. The Royal Commission, in recommending the introduction of MHRTs, considered that "the only satisfactory arrangement would be for the justification for the patient's detention in hospital or control under guardianship to be reviewed by some local body which could itself reassess the case from both medical and non-medical points of view".* Tribunals were therefore set up with medical, legal and lay members. To deny them the power to discharge, if necessary against the advice of the responsible medical officer, would thus be to deny them their prime function. It would also imply that the responsible medical officer's judgement of the need for continued detention is always the most reliable and assumes that he will always discharge a patient as soon as he should. The Mental Health Review Tribunal is the patient's main safeguard in that it provides an independent assessment of his detention. Errors of prognosis normally only come to light, of course, in relation to discharges subsequently found to have been made prematurely. Errors which involve patients being detained longer than necessary rarely come to public notice.

8.13 It has been suggested by many that the "all or nothing" nature of the options open to Tribunals places them in a difficult position and may have been a factor in cases in which discharged patients have subsequently committed serious offences. It must however be stressed that these are rare occurrences and that in such a difficult field as the prediction of future dangerousness it must be accepted that, whatever precautions are taken, there are likely to be occasional "failures" if large numbers of people are not to be detained unnecessarily. The Aarvold Committee said in their Report on offender patients subject to restriction under section 65:

> "The discharge and continuing care of mentally disordered offenders entails, fundamentally, the assessment and prediction, by one group of human beings, of the probable future behaviour of another. Prescribed procedures cannot offer real safeguards against the chance of human error going undetected, but we do not believe that in this sort of situation there can be an absolute guarantee of infallibility. Indeed there might be a risk that the adoption of over elaborate procedures could reduce the quality of judgements made by weakening the sense of personal responsibility which those who care for these unfortunate individuals lend to their task. The complete elimination of any risks to the public could only be achieved by continuing to detain these patients perhaps indefinitely, long after many of them had recovered from their mental disorder, and for periods in excess of any term of imprisonment they might have served as sentences for their offences. We are sure that in our society this would be seen as an inhumane avoidance of the responsibility for making a proper judgement in each case."**

8.14 All the bodies that have reported on the Act have however suggested extending the powers of Tribunals to enable them to do more than choose simply between absolute discharge and continued detention:

(a) The Butler Committee have recommended that Tribunals should adjourn hearings until they are satisfied that, as far as is practicable, suitable after-care arrangements have been made.***

---

* Cmnd 169: paragraph 442.
** Cmnd 5191: paragraph 57.
*** Cmnd 6244: paragraph 7.10.

(*b*) The Royal College of Psychiatrists have suggested that Tribunals should be empowered to specify a need for further supervision in the community and that prior to discharge the hospital staff should be made responsible both for prescribing the type of care needed and for ensuring that the necessary facilities are available.

(*c*) MIND have suggested that Tribunals should have all the powers of a legal guardian including

(i) full detention in hospital;
(ii) conditional discharge from hospital;
(iii) discharge to a community orientated treatment facility;
(iv) discharge into the care of a local authority;
(v) delayed discharge to enable proper after-care arrangements to be made;
(vi) transfer from a Special Hospital to a local hospital;
(vii) trial leave of absence.*

(*d*) The Council on Tribunals have recommended that Tribunals should have power to transfer or recommend transfer from one hospital to another more suited to the patients needs.

(*e*) The Chairmen of Tribunals consider that Tribunals should have power to make discharge conditional; that one or more social workers should be attached to a Tribunal in order to follow up conditionally discharged patients; and that a Tribunal should be able to adjourn a hearing in order to obtain the opinion of a psychiatrist from a local hospital to which they wish to transfer a Special Hospital patient or to discuss the matter with a psychiatrist who refuses to take the patient.

8.15 The Butler Committee received evidence that some Tribunals did not ensure that appropriate after-care arrangements had been made before they ordered the discharge of a patient. This seemed to be due to the fact that they interpreted Section 123 of the Act as requiring them to discharge the patient immediately. The precipitate discharge of a patient who has no home to go to is obviously undesirable. However, the solution proposed by the Committee, that Tribunals should exercise their existing power to adjourn hearings to enable arrangements including, for example, accommodation arrangements to be made, would not seem to provide a complete answer to this problem, since in those regions where this is done at present, experience shows that authorities are sometimes reluctant to make any definite arrangements without a firm discharge order. A better solution might be to enable a Tribunal to direct that a patient be discharged on or before some future date to allow time for appropriate after-care arrangements to be made. Three months might be a suitable period to enable, for example, accommodation to be obtained. If such a power were given it would presumably have to be made clear that the patient should cease to be detained at the notified future date whether or not fully satisfactory after-care arrangements have been made. This might go some way towards meeting the criticism made by the Scottish Mental Welfare Commission that patients are sometimes detained simply because they have "no place to go".

* A Human Condition: Vol I pages 63–64.

8.16 More generally, there seems merit in the idea of giving Tribunals a wider range of powers as to disposal. It is, however, important to distinguish between ordering a disposal and recommending one. As the Chairmen themselves recognise, there would be difficulty in enabling them to order, for example, a transfer since this could only be effected with the co-operation of the receiving authority. For some disposals a recommendation would therefore be more suitable. On the other hand, it is clearly right that a recommendation should carry considerable weight, and a Tribunal should be able to require reasons to be given if their recommendation is not implemented.

8.17 The sort of disposal options which might be provided could include all of those suggested by MIND. The Tribunals should be able only to recommend a transfer to another hospital or to the care of a local authority since this arrangement must depend upon mutual agreement and upon the type of facilities available. A recommendation would also be appropriate in the case of trial leave of absence as the responsibility for the behaviour of the patient during that period would rest upon the responsible medical officer whose views might well not accord with the Tribunal's decision. Conditional discharge would also have to be a matter for recommendation since a Tribunal, being an *ad hoc* body constituted only to hear the cases put before it, could not be responsible for supervision and control: this would be for the hospital staff to arrange. Similarly it would not be practicable to adopt the MIND suggestion that a Tribunal should have the powers of a legal guardian.

8.18 Another suggestion is that an application should not be withdrawn without the permission of the Tribunal and that, if withdrawn before being heard, it should not prevent a further application being made within the specified period. This seems acceptable.

8.19 MIND have suggested that there should be a social work member on each Tribunal and the Butler Committee with the support of the Chairmen of Tribunals have advised that forensic psychiatrists should be among the medical members. Such additions would appear to provide a useful widening of expertise. It has also been suggested that it would help to ensure that the Tribunal was not only independent but seen to be independent if the medical members were drawn from another Region, but this might increase the pressures on medical manpower mentioned in paragraph 8.10 above.

Consent to treatment

8.20 The right of the responsible medical officer to impose treatment on an unwilling patient, whether detained or not, has not so far been tested in court. The Royal Commission* took the view that Society had the right to impose treatment on a mentally disordered patient against his will and it follows from this that they considered that it ought to be possible to override his refusal. The view of the Department of Health and Social Security's legal advisers is that the 1959 Act gives the responsible medical officer the authority to treat a detained patient but does not require him to seek the consent of any other person. Nevertheless the Department's advice to those doctors who seek it is, if possible, to obtain the consent of both the patient and the nearest relative

---

* Cmnd 169: paragraph 316.

(although the latter has no validity in law) before beginning a form of treatment which involves any risks. The Medical Defence Union have received similar legal advice and this is contained in their booklet "Consent to Treatment".

8.21 The Royal College of Psychiatrists, the Butler Committee, MIND and the Davies Committee have all indicated that they feel some improvement in the position to be necessary. The Royal College have suggested that for those patients unable or unwilling to give consent to treatment a code of practice should be followed which would involve consulting and, where possible obtaining the agreement of their next of kin, recording this agreement or otherwise, and obtaining an independent consultant psychiatric opinion in writing. The final decision about the treatment of the patient would, however, rest with the responsible medical officer who should record his reasons for carrying out the treatment, especially if the opinion of the independent consultant was against this. The Davies Committee have recommended* that a second and independent medical opinion should be obtained in any decision to impose treatment on a detained mental patient. The Butler Committee and MIND have both made more comprehensive and far-reaching proposals. In relation to offenders, the Butler Committee recommend** that if a patient is unable to give a valid consent to treatment the doctor should be able to give him treatment which is not irreversible or hazardous; but where the proposed treatment is irreversible or hazardous he should obtain a second opinion and consult the patient's relatives before deciding whether or not to proceed. In the case of a patient who is able to give a valid consent but refuses to do so, only the minimum treatment necessary in order to prevent his being a danger to himself or others (not being hazardous or irreversible), to save life, or to prevent him from deteriorating (not being irreversible) should be given. If the patient is able to consent and does so a proposal to provide irreversible or hazardous treatment should be accompanied by a second opinion and consultation with the relatives. (See paragraph 8.24 below). MIND suggest*** that a patient should be asked to give an informed voluntary consent to a particular treatment. If he does not, or if he does but the treatment is one which "irreversibly or unpredictably affects the patient"—what MIND call "suspect" treatment—an arbitration mechanism in the form of a Committee on the Rights and Responsibilities of Staff and Residents of Psychiatric Hospitals (CORR) should be used to decide whether or not treatment of the kind in question should be imposed in the circumstances. If the Committee considers that the patient's refusal is informed and responsible the treatment should not be given.

8.22 The Butler Committee, MIND and the Royal College of Psychiatrists are thus in agreement that irreversible and hazardous treatment should be distinguished from other forms of treatment although the Royal College confines its recommendations to cases in which the patient does not agree to the treatment proposed. In the light of suggestions made elsewhere in this document (paragraphs 1.27–1.28) that compulsory admission to hospital should be more closely related to the prospect of benefit from treatment and that, except in specific cases, detention should not be continued without an affirmation that

* Report of the Committee on Hospital Complaints Procedure 1973: paragraph 7.36.
** Cmnd 6244: paragraphs 3.54–3.59.
*** A Human Condition: Vol I pages 116 and 117

the patient is likely to benefit from further treatment, it would not seem possible to consider the issue of consent to treatment without reference to the fact that the need for in-patient treatment was the reason for admission to hospital in the first instance. In other words, all patients in a psychiatric hospital except those admitted for observation and assessment should be expected to receive treatment, at least in the first stages of their stay and this needs to be regarded as a necessary adjunct to admission to hospital, whether the admission is compulsory or voluntary. In the case of an informal patient, the position is relatively clear in that if he does not consent to the treatment proposed or to any alternative treatments which might be available, he may choose as a last resort to leave the hospital. In the case of the compulsorily detained patient, the position is more complex: he may not wish to receive a particular form of treatment but he is unable to discharge himself. The position of the hospital staff is also difficult since their function is treatment, with detention if necessary to achieve this, but not detention without treatment. While it seems unreasonable that any patient who enters hospital either voluntarily or compulsorily should be allowed to refuse all forms of treatment, it does not necessarily follow that either type of patient must submit to *any* form of treatment proposed for him. As has been pointed out by the Butler Committee, MIND and others, there are some forms of treatment which carry risks and others which result in irreversible changes and, while it may be reasonable to insist that a patient take a tranquillising drug to prevent him from injuring himself or others, it is another matter to insist that he undergo, for example, brain surgery for the same reason. Similarly it may be acceptable to insist upon a patient receiving a well established form of treatment but not one which has not been so established or is controversial.

PATIENTS WHO ARE COMPULSORILY DETAINED

Treatment Without Consent

8.23 There seems to be general agreement that some clarification of the position relating to treatment without consent would be welcomed. The Butler Committee have put forward a formula which goes some way to cover the situations in which treatment would be imposed:

> "Treatment (other than nursing care) should not be imposed on any patient without his consent if he is able to appreciate what is involved. Three exceptions should be allowed: treatment may be given without such a patient's consent:
>
> (*a*) where (not being of a hazardous or irreversible character) it represents the minimum interference with the patient to prevent him from behaving violently or otherwise being a danger to himself or others; or
>
> (*b*) where it is necessary to save the patient's life; or
>
> (*c*) where (not being irreversible) it is necessary to prevent him from deteriorating.
>
> Where by reason of his disability the patient is unable to appreciate what is involved, despite the help of an explanation in simple terms, the treatment may be given: but special considerations apply to treatment involving irreversible procedures."*

---

* Cmnd 6244: paragraph 3.54.

The question of irreversible procedures is discussed in paragraphs 8.24–8.27 below. Although the Mental Health Act is thought to provide powers to override the common law right of a patient to refuse treatment it is doubtful whether it would generally be considered right to do this with respect to more radical forms of treatment. The Butler Committee formula does seem to strike the right balance. It was put forward in relation to mentally disordered offenders but would be equally applicable to non-offender detained patients.

"Irreversible or Hazardous" Treatment

8.24 The Butler Committee went on to suggest* that the types of treatment which it referred to as "hazardous or irreversible" should not be used, even if the patient had given his consent, without a second psychiatric opinion independent of the treating hospital or prison being obtained unless the delay would cause or increase a danger to life. If possible the nearest relative should be consulted. The Committee explained that "by 'hazardous or irreversible' procedures we mean those entailing immediate significant physical hazard or having unfavourable irreversible physical or psychological consequences".** They argued in their report that consent to such treatment might be influenced by the patient's feelings that his chances of discharge would be increased by accepting the treatment and that, given these pressures on a patient, there was a need for an extra safeguard in relation to irreversible procedures. If there is substance in this argument, the extra safeguard would be helpful both from the patient's and the doctor's point of view. The Committee did not make it clear whether they felt it necessary for the second opinion to agree with the first before the procedure was carried out. Certainly the Royal College of Psychiatrists have suggested that this need not be the case since, in the College's view, only the responsible medical officer can take the final decision about treatment, particularly if he does not accept the opinion of the independent consultant. It is not thought, however, that public opinion would regard the obtaining of a second opinion as a safeguard if the responsible medical officer could disregard it.

8.25 Certain difficulties may be foreseen in obtaining an independent psychiatric second opinion. It may be thought by some that this might deteriorate into a mere formality or at least that another doctor would be unwilling to question a colleague's clinical judgement. These may be reasons for considering whether a second opinion should be a medical one or whether the views of other professionals might not be sought. The recent discussion about the proposed sterilisation of a girl described by Mrs Justice Heilbron as "mentally backward" has shown that other professionals and the public do not always accept that decisions as to whether a particular medical treatment should be used should always be left entirely to doctors, especially when the treatment is proposed for social reasons or is based, at least in part, on a non-medical prognosis. The increasing involvement of members of other professions such as psychologists and nurses in the treatment of patients, for example by behaviour modification, may add weight to the argument that the second opinion need not be a psychiatric one. On the other hand it would be extremely difficult for legislation to point out which other profession should be involved since this is likely to vary according to the circumstances of the individual case.

---

* Cmnd 6244: paragraph 3.56.
** Ibid: page 49 footnote.

8.26 Instead of a second opinion MIND has suggested that a Committee on the Rights and Responsibilities of Staff and Residents of Psychiatric Hospitals which they recommend as part of an advocacy system (see paragraphs 8.44–8.47) should also deal with issues relating to what they call "suspect treatment". They propose that such Committees should be set up by the Lord Chancellor's Department nationally and in each region with between five and ten members representing a wide range of views. Although this machinery would seem cumbersome and elaborate there may be a case for modifying it for this particular use. Indeed a similar proposal has been suggested in the Department of Health and Social Security Discussion Paper on the Sterilisation of Children under 16 which included, as one alternative approach, a proposal for:

> "A statutory requirement that sterilisation should be approved by an independent local "ethical" committee with lay as well as professional membership—set up perhaps by the Area Health Authority."*

8.27 In the psychiatric field, multidisciplinary panels could be established with such functions as:

(i) providing a second opinion whenever it is proposed to carry out treatment which is irreversible, hazardous or which has not yet been fully established, whether the patient has consented or is not capable of giving a valid consent;

(ii) giving advice in any other case in which the doctor feels it would be helpful, for example on whether or not a form of treatment should be considered irreversible, hazardous or not fully established ;

(iii) considering complaints by individual patients that they are not receiving adequate treatment: this would go some way to meeting MIND's point about the need to ensure the patient's "right to treatment".

In the light of the functions which were to be carried out, the number of cases which would go to the panel etc, it would need to be decided whether these should be established at hospital, at Area Health Authority, or at Regional Health Authority level.

Patients Admitted for Observation and Assessment (*Section* 25)

8.28 As has been pointed out above, there is a lack of clarity as to whether treatment, other than observation and assessment can be imposed on patients who are detained under section 25. The MIND Report argues that the provisions of the section are ambiguous and says:

> "In the case of admission for "observation" or "emergency observation", it would have to be maintained that the restrictions of compulsory detention are all inclusive, and so include the power to impose treatment. Despite the obvious uncertainties of interpretation, hospital authorities have assumed this power and the courts have not been called upon to judge the issue".**

8.29 Whilst it seems fairly clear that it may be necessary to impose some form of treatment on a patient detained under section 25 or 29 in order to deal with the emergency situation which lead to his admission insofar as

---

* Enclosed with DS/333/75.
** A Human Condition: Vol I page 122.

this is necessary to save his life or to prevent him being violent, it is less clear that forms of treatment geared to the longer term situation should be imposed without the patient's consent. In cases where a form of treatment is felt to be required in order to, for example, prevent the deterioration of the patient or to arrest the development of his illness, but where his consent to this cannot be obtained, it would seem more appropriate to use the powers of detention for treatment under section 26 than to use section 25 as, in effect, authority for short term treatment. If section 25 is used in this way in practice, rather than as a period of assessment of the need for detention for treatment, this has serious implications since less stringent criteria attach to a section 25 admission in terms of the diagnosis of the disorder and content of the medical recommendations than apply in the case of an application under section 26. There is also, as MIND point out, no right of appeal to a MHRT for a patient detained for observation. If it were possible to impose treatment on such a patient, not only to save his life or prevent him from being violent, but also to prevent him from deteriorating, consideration would have to be given to the introduction of a procedure whereby he could appeal against such treatment. However a limitation of the treatment permitted by section 25 would seem to be preferable.

INFORMAL PATIENTS—CONSENT TO TREATMENT

8.30 The above discussion has related to detained patients, whether offenders or not, for whom some degree of protection seems required as far as certain types of treatment are concerned. The informal patient is less in need of this sort of protection since it is open to him, as a last resort, to leave the hospital if he does not wish to receive the form of treatment proposed. It seems reasonable to assume that any patient who enters the hospital informally should be prepared to receive treatment within the formula suggested by the Butler Committee ie that described in paragraph 8.21. If, however, a patient refused a form of treatment which was considered essential for his health or for the protection of others the proper course would be to seek to use the compulsory powers of detention under section 30 and then section 26 before treatment was given rather than to attempt to impose it against his will as an informal patient.

8.31 However, some informal patients are incapable of understanding explanations about proposed treatment and others may believe that if they do not consent they will be formally detained and receive the treatment anyway. In the light of this it would seem helpful to extend the protection suggested for detained patients in paragraph 8.27 in relation to hazardous or irreversible treatment to informal patients, even where they have consented to the treatment.

IMPLEMENTATION

8.32 If there were general support for changes of this kind, the best means of achieving these would need to be decided. The Butler Committee appear to be suggesting that there should be a legislative basis for the change whilst the Royal College of Psychiatrists have suggested a professional code of practice.

A Code of Practice?

8.33 If only a code of practice were to be used, it would seem necessary for this to be produced, or at least agreed, on a multi-professional basis and for it both to define the forms of treatment for which a second opinion is required, ie those that are hazardous, irreversible or not yet established, and to give guidance in considering individual cases. There would also need to be a mechanism for considering new forms of treatment as they became available or other methods as they became established. If, however, a less specific protection were thought adequate it would be possible for a code to be produced in general terms without specifying individual forms of treatment.

8.34 A code of practice would probably be less of a safeguard for patients than a legislative solution. It would also be unlikely to be widely available, or meaningful, to the general public and would leave patients in some uncertainty with regard to consent.

Legislation?

8.35 If the Butler Committee formula were to be included in legislation together with the need to obtain a second opinion in the case of treatment which did not fall within the scope of that formula, this would be a considerable extra safeguard for patients. There would be broadly three alternative ways in which this might be done:

(i) To identify the "hazardous" treatments and to update a list of these on a regular basis. One means of doing this would be to draw up a list in a schedule to a statutory instrument with the help of an advisory body; new treatments could be added to the list and old ones removed from it if they met the broad criteria laid down in the Act.

(ii) To incorporate the basic requirements into the legislation and to supplement this with a professional code of practice accompanied by a list of these treatments; the list would, however, also need regular updating.

(iii) To incorporate the Butler formula in the Act, without attempting to identify specific treatments, and to leave the clarification of the position with respect to particular treatment to the court if necessary.

8.36 Alternative (i) above would require the setting up of an advisory committee and the regular notification of changes in the list to field authorities, but it is not thought that such changes are likely to be made frequently or that the task would be an onerous one, once the initial list had been drawn up. Although possibly providing firmer protection for patients, it would be administratively cumbersome. Alternative (ii) above would have the disadvantage, for patients and staff alike, of being less authoritative than a statutory list and would have considerable administrative implications. Alternative (iii) would be the least precise but would be much simpler. The judgement of courts on particular treatments would have the advantage of being able to take account of the particular circumstances at the time. In practice the need for court hearings would no doubt be very limited. The disadvantage of this alternative is that uncertainty would continue until a body of case law had been established and this might take many years.

8.37 Whilst the philosophy behind the recommendations by the Butler Committee seems right, and whilst there are several ways of giving effect to these, careful thought would need to be given to the likely end results before it were decided to opt for one of these solutions. There may be some counter-balancing of the advantages if doctors were to feel so restricted as to be reluctant to provide treatment which would be of benefit to their patients. A further alternative would be to give general endorsement to the Butler Committee proposals in Departmental guidance and to rely on the good judgment and goodwill of staff and patients in co-operating in arrangements for treatment within that broad framework.

Other suggestions for improving the protection of the patient

MENTAL WELFARE COMMISSIONS

8.38 The Royal College of Psychiatrists have suggested that commissions similar to the Mental Welfare Commission of Scotland should be established in England and Wales since they regret that the Board of Control was not replaced by a body of comparable functions. The Scottish Mental Welfare Commission was created under section 2 of the Mental Health (Scotland) Act 1960 and consists of not less than 7 and not more than 11 commissioners of whom 1 is Chairman, at least 1 a woman, at least 3 medical practitioners and 1 a lawyer. Two full-time medical commissioners along with the Commission's medical officers, do much of the day-to-day work of the Commission and undertake most of the routine visits to hospitals. The functions and duties of the Commission are set out in section 4 of the Act (see Appendix VI) and their primary duty is "generally to exercise protective functions in respect of persons who may, by reason of mental disorder, be incapable of adequately protecting their persons or their interests".

8.39 The Scottish Mental Welfare Commission is a body with strong medical representation and with good contact at all levels, and in all areas. One of its strengths lies in its ability to look into a problem or complaint with whatever degree of formality it believes to be appropriate in a particular case, ranging from a very informal approach to a quasi-judicial enquiry with evidence on oath. The presence of an independent body able to adopt a flexible approach and to deal with complaints of any degree of magnitude at an early stage, it is argued, may have prevented the development of the sorts of situations which have led elsewhere to demands for public enquiries. Obviously there are advantages to be gained from an informal, yet independent investigation of certain individual complaints, but the avoidance of *ad hoc* full-scale enquiries resulting in published reports is not necessarily an unmixed blessing. The publication of such reports can perhaps provide valuable lessons for the service as a whole and help to bring home to the general public the problems which can arise from shortages of staff and resources. Although it would be possible for commissions to publish reports which are critical of some aspects of particular institutions, it may be thought that they could be inhibited in doing so by their need to maintain a good relationship with the institution on a continuing basis. An *ad hoc* enquiry might seem less likely to be affected by such a constraint and is also less in danger of being identified with the "establishment". The other main advantage of the Commission is the interest it is able to take in individual patients and their problems and complaints. In this it overlaps, to an extent, with the functions performed in England and Wales by the Court of Protection and Lord Chancellor's Visitors. If commissions were established in England and Wales it would thus be necessary to consider the extent to which they would take over these functions.

8.40 Since the advantages of the Scottish Commission are thought to be largely due to close contact and co-operation with field authorities and to mutual understanding and respect, it would be necessary, in England and Wales, to have a commission for each health region if similar close relations were to be built up. Such a development would have significant manpower and resource implications since, if commissions were to be established on the same lines as that in Scotland, 30 full-time staff would be required. If these were taken from the medical field as in Scotland, this would be an additional drain on manpower in the psychiatric field where there are already shortages. Even if more use of other professions such as social work were to be made, as some would certainly argue should be the case, this would still be a problem since there are manpower shortages in these also. The financial implications would be significant. It is estimated that regional commissions and one in Wales would cost about £1½m per year (plus the cost of accommodation).

8.41 There are other drawbacks. The Scottish Commission being strongly medically based, part of its accepted remit is to question, though on an informal basis, the clinical judgement of the doctors in the hospitals it visits. It might be difficult to get such a policy accepted in England and Wales, where developments in the last 15 years or so have been rather different. Were commissions to be introduced in England and Wales, it would seem necessary for them to be established on a multi-professional basis and for there to be representation by nursing and social work members as well as medical members: there is some development on these lines already in Scotland. This would make the role and position of the commission with respect to the questioning of clinical judgement an even more complex one, though more in keeping with the current concept of the multi-disciplinary therapeutic team. In order to carry out this function the staff of the commission would need to be of high calibre. It may be doubted whether such people would be attracted to this kind of work in sufficient numbers, or whether the clinical services could stand up to such a drain on their resources.

8.42 As outlined in paragraph 8.2 above, there have been a number of developments since the 1959 Act which would overlap with the functions of mental welfare commissions if these were introduced. Some of these, for example, Community Health Councils and the development of a code of practice on complaints procedures, relate to all health service patients, not solely the mentally disordered, and there is thought to be considerable advantage in bringing the mentally disordered into the main-stream of these procedures wherever possible, rather than isolating them by the continuation of separate arrangements. There may, on the other hand, be a case for topping up the usual procedures by additional protection for especially vulnerable groups, such as the mentally handicapped and mentally ill, and this is discussed in paragraph 8.48 below. Commissions on the lines of the Scottish Commission may be thought to provide too paternalistic a solution to this problem and, as direct heirs to the old Board of Control, might be thought to be out of keeping with the multi-professional and community policies of today. Such commissions might also be viewed as an extension of the "establishment", particularly in view of the necessary professional participation, and their independence might be suspect.

"GUARDIANS" OR PATIENTS' FRIENDS

8.43 The Butler Committee recommended* that statutory provision should be made to allow the appointment of "guardians" for patients detained under the restrictions set out in section 65 of the Act. The provision would be on the same lines as section 24 (5) of the Children and Young Persons Act 1969. Under this section the local authority has a duty to appoint a visitor for a child who has been confined in a community home or other establishment for over 3 months and who has little or no contact with his parent or guardian. The duties of the visitor are to visit, advise and befriend the child, and to apply to a juvenile court on his behalf for a discharge order if this is appropriate. The Butler Committee recognised the difficulties in finding sufficient numbers of people of the right calibre to take an interest in this work and they therefore only recommended that it should be made possible for people to be appointed to this role, not that it should be mandatory for them to be so appointed. These problems would, of course, be multiplied considerably if the suggestion were to be extended to patients other than those under section 65 restriction orders.

PROPOSAL FOR AN ADVOCACY SYSTEM

8.44 MIND**, on the other hand, have suggested a considerable extension to the arrangements for the protection of rights of patients, both those detained and those receiving treatment on an informal basis. The comprehensive system which they envisage would consist of:

(i) a minimum of one advocate at each institution (or one advocate for every 500 residents of the institution).
(ii) an advocacy co-ordinator, ie a lawyer at regional or national level.
(iii) a quasi-judicial system of Committees on the Rights and Responsibilities of Staff and Residents of Psychiatric Hospitals (CORRs) at both institutional and national levels, to consider difficult issues raised by advocates and other interested parties.

8.45 Advocates would not need to have any specific qualifications but should come from a relevant background. Their function would be "to monitor violations of residents rights, advise or educate staff and residents when rights are being violated, advocate the resident's position before CORR, and residents, staff, parents and guardians on legal rights, and the reasons for extending or limiting their rights".

8.46 The idea is for a largely legal system under the direct supervision of the Lord Chancellor's Department: this, in MIND's view, would redress the balance which the 1959 Act tilted too much towards the medical profession and away from the general issues of civil liberties and rights.

---

* Cmnd 6244: paragraphs 7.26–7.28.
** A Human Condition: Vol I pages 130–135.

8.47 Whatever the view on the present balance between these, the suggested system would be a very complicated one to introduce and maintain and, although there are certainly defects in the existing system to which this Document draws attention, it seems doubtful whether an advocacy system on this scale is called for.

PATIENTS' ADVISERS

8.48 Whilst it may be preferable for the same arrangements to apply generally to the mentally disordered as to other patients, there would seem to be a place for some additional protection for this particularly vulnerable group. Any such additional protection would need to be responsive to local variations in services and problems and would need to be sufficiently accessible to individual patients to minimise the problems which MIND, among others, have pointed out, of informing patients of their rights and how to exercise them. One way of meeting this need on a fairly informal basis might be to introduce a scheme of "patients' advisers" for those in hospitals or other residential accommodation or attending as out-patients or day-patients. Their existence could be advertised locally in order to make them known to mentally disordered people in the community or those in contact with them. The main function of the "advisers" would be to advise the mentally disordered about their rights generally and about procedural matters, for example, the formal complaints procedures. They could bring any wider issues or deficiencies to the attention of the CHC or local authority as appropriate. From this point of view it might be thought helpful if these advisers could be employed on behalf of each CHC (if each CHC had one adviser this would mean approximately 200 advisers in all). However, CHCs themselves cannot employ staff: the staff made available to CHCs are employees of the health authorities, although entirely at the disposal of CHCs and, since it would seem important in any event that these advisers should be independent of the health authorities, this may be considered to be a drawback. An alternative to employment on behalf of the CHCs would be for them to be provided by voluntary agencies on a grant-aided basis. From this point of view it is interesting to note the scheme which started in May at Pitsmoor Hospital, Sheffield run as an information and advice centre jointly by the local Citizen's Advice Bureau and the hospital's social workers. With respect to the proposal outlined above there may be room for co-operation between the voluntary bodies and CHCs in setting up such arrangements. Whilst expertise and experience would be assets in the people concerned, it would seem more important that those chosen should be concerned for the rights of patients than that they should possess particular skills. It may, in any case, be advisable to exclude the use of such people as nurses or social workers who might tend to identify with the institution or service. Advisers would presumably need to be allowed to visit hospitals and other institutions without prior arrangement and, on occasion, to work from a base in a particular institution.

8.49 If a development of this kind was thought to be generally helpful, DHSS would be prepared to consider its funding on an experimental basis and would discuss the details of any such project with the other bodies which might need to be involved. Comments would be welcome.

CHAPTER 9. PROTECTION OF STAFF

9.1 Statutory provisions which involve removing a person to hospital, detaining him there and imposing medical treatment on him against his will, carry a risk that those responsible for operating the procedures may be faced with legal action initiated by patients or ex-patients arising out of actions taken in the course of their duties. Mental health legislation has, therefore, traditionally included some provision for the protection of those operating the statute.* Section 330 of the Lunacy Act of 1890 enabled any proceedings against staff to be stayed upon summary application to the High Court or one of its Judges if they were satisfied that there were no reasonable grounds for alleging want of good faith or reasonable care. In practice this meant that the defendant had to show the Court that he acted in good faith and with reasonable care before the proceedings could be stayed.

9.2 The Mental Treatment Act 1930 reinforced this by requiring substantial grounds to be shown for alleging that the action was carried out in bad faith or without reasonable care and also made it necessary for the plantiff to seek leave from the High Court before proceeding. Protection thus was no longer dependent on the defendant applying for a stay of proceedings. Reporting in 1957, the Royal Commission recommended that:

> "The substance of section 16 of the Mental Treatment Act 1930 (which affords protection from legal proceedings for persons who take part in certification or other procedures unless they have acted in bad faith or without reasonable care) should be re-enacted in the new legislation and should apply in proceedings arising from any action, report or recommendations made in connection with the new compulsory proceedings".**

This protection is provided in section 141 of the 1959 Act and extends to all those performing functions purporting to be carried out under the Act.

9.3 Section 141 is concerned only with the protection of individuals personally against legal proceedings for alleged wrongs. The section does not, therefore, affect the right of a patient or his friends to apply to the High Court at any time for discharge by means of a writ of *habeas corpus,* so that the lawfulness or otherwise of his detention can be tested. It may be worth pointing out however that MIND have argued***, in the context of section 29 admissions, that the Courts are unlikely to question the medical judgement of the doctor and that such applications are only likely to succeed if the procedure of admission is in some way technically faulty.

9.4 A recent case which went to the House of Lords, R v Bracknell Justices ex parte Griffiths**** made it clear that section 141, apart from covering actions specifically described in the Act, also extended to the control of detained patients. In this case, a Broadmoor Hospital nurse, having been convicted of common assault, appealed to the High Court on the ground that his action,

---

* As well as hospital staff, this includes, for example, the nearest relative, a police constable, mental welfare officer and family practitioner.

** Cmnd 169: paragraph 490.

*** A Human Condition: Vol I page 30.

**** 1975 3 WLR 140.

being part of his duty in controlling the patient, should have been protected by section 141. The High Court agreed as did the House of Lords on appeal. In the House of Lords judgement, Lord Edmund Davies said:

> "The conception of detention and treatment necessarily implies that the staff of the hospital, including the male nurses, can and on occasion must, use reasonable force in order to ensure that control is exercised over the patient".

9.5 There are, however, three other areas of doubt which the judgement did not cover, namely treatment of detained patients, treatment of informal patients and control of informal patients. Although the Act provides for the compulsory admission of a patient for treatment on the grounds that "the said disorder is of a nature or degree which warrants the detention of the patient in a hospital for medical treatment" (including nursing, and care and training under medical supervision) it is not clear whether such treatment is provided in pursuance of the Mental Health Act or under the general powers and duties to provide treatment in the National Health Service Acts. If it is provided in pursuance of the Mental Health Act it clearly falls within the compass of section 141. But even if detained patients are deemed to receive treatment under the Mental Health Act, it may still be held that informal patients do not and that section 141 does not therefore apply to them. The uncertainty with relation to the control of informal patients was illustrated by the report of the Inquiry into the Death of a Nurse at Tooting Bec Hospital which made it clear that the nurses were not sufficiently confident of their position in law and indicated that some clarification was desirable. Uncertainties of this sort are not helpful at a time when staff are in any case showing increasing reluctance to deal with difficult patients, especially those for whom some form of physical restraint may on occasion be needed. The opinion of Treasury Counsel has been sought on the extent of the protection afforded by section 141 in relation to these three areas of doubt.

9.6 Apart from these doubts, other criticisms have been expressed concerning the degree of protection afforded by this section. MIND holds the view that it provides too much protection from staff to the detriment of patients, many of whom are unable to defend their own interests; whereas the main concern of the staff in psychiatric hospitals is that it is not clear which actions are covered. The discussion which follows aims to set out the arguments which have been put forward for removing section 141 or reducing the protection which it provides for those operating the legislation, and to point to the problems related to this with a view to seeking opinions on what the scope of this protection should be. Once opinions have been received it will be possible to compare what is generally felt to be required with what is already covered according to the Treasury Counsels opinion.

9.7 MIND's comments are more far-reaching than those of other groups. They argue that admission to hospital should not, of itself, involve the loss of normal access to the courts as implied by the House of Lords judgement in the Pountney v Griffiths case and that section 141 "is a prophylactic approach to a problem which is supported more in prejudgement than in fact".*

---

* A Human Condition: Vol I page 110.

They point out that the majority of psychiatric inpatients are likely to be too helpless through illness or mental handicap to consider taking legal action and that there is, in any case, already a procedure for requiring a person who persistently brings vexatious actions to seek leave for any further litigation. This procedure is based on past behaviour which MIND believes to be "the only predictor accurate enough to curtail the fundamental right of access to the Courts."* (It is also possible for any action to be stopped if, once the proceedings have begun, the Court finds it to be vexatious). MIND further argue that even if one accepts the need for some kind of screening, section 141 goes too far in protecting the person from being proceeded against even "on the ground of want of jurisdiction or on any other ground" (in other words for carrying out an action which the Act gives him no right to carry out—see paragraph 9.8 below) and also in requiring the High Court to find "*substantial* ground for the contention that the person to be proceeded against acted in bad faith or without reasonable care". See paragraph 9.9 below.

9.8 It is certainly true that few applications for leave under section 141 are made—4 in 1970, 1 in 1971, 3 in 1972, 7 in 1973, (5 by the same person), 4 in 1974 and 5 in 1975—but whether this is because few patients wish to bring proceedings or because solicitors advise against doing so because section 141 is thought to provide such comprehensive protection, is not known. The purpose of including within the section's protection those who acted without jurisdiction was to prevent proceedings being brought against a person who acted on the basis of, for example, a technically invalid medical recommendation and was thus implicated in the illegal detention of the patient but without knowing that it was illegal. The Protection of Constables Act 1750 provided similar protection for constables acting in good faith on the basis of a false warrant. Whilst protecting a person in this situation, section 141 also seems to protect a person who acts on the belief that the Act says something which it does not say, except where the plaintiff can show substantial ground for the contention that the action was performed without reasonable care or in bad faith.

9.9 One of the risks of including in the Act a protection of this kind is that it may in practice be difficult to show *substantial* grounds for bad faith and lack of reasonable care. The section may also act as a bar to proceedings being taken against persons who, although not acting in bad faith or without reasonable care, nevertheless act in such a way as to jeopardise the patient's interests. Section 141 appears to preclude court action for damages for wrongful admission to hospital or guardianship (except where there is bad faith or a lack of reasonable care) and also covers the actions of staff in controlling patients, even, presumably, if such actions are not in accordance with good professional practice and infringe on the rights of patients to a greater extent than is necessary. If the courts were to decide that psychiatric treatment was carried out under the Mental Health Act, the section would also cover a doctor in all his professional actions unless he acted negligently or in bad faith. It relates not only to civil, but also to criminal proceedings unless these fall within the scope of those sections of the Act designed to provide specific

* A Human Condition: Vol. I, page 110

protection for the patient from offences by staff in well defined areas—section 125, forgery and false statements, section 126, neglect and ill treatment, and sections 127 and 128, sexual offences—or there is evidence of deliberate misconduct. It is certainly arguable, therefore, that section 141 is too comprehensive and that patients may be at too great a disadvantage because of it.

9.10 The difficulty of lessening the protection afforded by this section is that this may have an adverse effect on the way the professionals perform their statutory functions and on the day to day care of patients detained under the Act. It would be most unfortunate if, for example, doctors were inhibited from giving a patient treatment he urgently required for fear of legal action. Nurses might similarly become less willing to supervise those activities which may involve them coming into physical contact with patients and in using physical restraint if it becomes necessary. One of the most difficult areas for staff is the exercise of sensible precautions designed to prevent a patient, detained or informal, from doing harm to himself or others. A patient who is willing to enter and remain in hospital is admitted informally, no matter how seriously disturbed he may be. Some informal patients occasionally require physical restraint which the staff must feel able to use provided it accords with good professional practice, without fear of being taken to court. The Department of Health Circular on the Management of Violent or Potentially Violent Hospital Patients,* is intended to reassure staff of the extent of their powers in this respect. Nurses are sometimes attacked by patients and this they normally accept, without retaliatory recourse to the courts, as part of the patient's illness. While not seeking to condone ill treatment or to be immune from punishment if it occurs, they naturally feel that if a nurse is to prevent a violent patient from doing harm to himself or others, he should be able to do so without the fear, provided he acts in good faith and in accordance with the training he has received, of being charged with assault. Restraint may also be necessary if on a sudden impulse a seriously disordered informal patient decides to leave hospital and here the proposal in paragraph 2.18 above to amend section 30 to enable action to be taken more quickly would help to reduce the period of uncertainty for both staff and patients.

9.11 Some means of protecting staff undertaking this difficult and demanding work from unjustified harrassment in the courts would seem to be needed. On the other hand the existing protection goes very wide, both in terms of procedure and of the actions covered, and some change might be helpful to staff and patients alike. A number of changes which might be made are outlined below; they are not mutually exclusive.

9.12 Administrative action might be taken to ensure that those responsible for operating the Act know more clearly what is expected of them, possibly through DHSS or professional guidance and clarification of the consent to treatment issues as discussed in paragraphs 8.20–8.27. This would help the Court to determine whether an action had or had not been performed in good faith or with reasonable care, since the action should accord with the practice laid down. The suggestion in paragraphs 2.10 and 2.30 that the forms used in admitting a patient should be changed to require more information to be supplied, should similarly give the Court a better base for making a judgement.

* HC(76)11.

9.13 Ways of reducing the scope of section 141 might be considered. For example:

(i) Criminal actions might be removed from within its scope, including actions for common assault, and made subject to the provisions of section 126, namely that the Director of Public Prosecutions should have to give leave for proceedings against staff to be taken. Under the section 141 proceedings, the High Court is unable to give leave unless satisfied of substantial grounds for the contention that the action was performed in bad faith or without reasonable care, whereas under section 126 the Director of Public Prosecutions considers each case on the particular facts of the case.

(ii) It would be possible to revert to the system which prevailed before the Mental Treatment Act 1930 whereby the onus was on the member of staff to make a summary application to the High Court for a stay of proceedings rather than on the patient to apply for leave to proceed. In making such an application the defendant would have to show the High Court that the plaintiff did not have reasonable grounds for asserting that he acted in bad faith or without reasonable care and to do this he would have to show that he acted in good faith and with reasonable care. In any case of doubt the case would normally be heard. However, in any attempt to increase the access of patients to the courts, it should be remembered that there will be a point at which the morale of staff might be damaged to such an extent that the proper application of treatment is inhibited. The benefit to the individual might therefore be given at the expense of patients and the community as a whole.

(iii) The word "substantial" might be removed from the section and the word "reasonable" substituted so that the patient only has to show that there is a case to answer. It is interesting to note that section 111 of the Mental Health (Northern Ireland) Act 1961 which is in other respects almost identical to section 141, has the words "prima facie case".

(iv) It might be possible to amend the section so that actions not performed in pursuance of the Act are not protected but it should be borne in mind that persons who had no reason to suspect that they had no jurisdiction in relation to a patient might thereby become liable to court proceedings.

9.14 It is thought that a combination of (i) and (iii) together with administrative action of the kind described in paragraph 9.12 would represent a significant improvement.

CHAPTER 10. PROTECTION OF THE PUBLIC

10.1 The power to detain in hospital or place under guardianship a mentally disordered person who has not come before the court depends on such action being either in the interests of his own health or safety or needed for the protection of others. The protection of others is clearly an important consideration and one which overrides most others if the patient is dangerous. A number of suggestions have been made in this paper for providing extra safeguards for patients and, in framing these, it has been recognised that changes could not be made which would increase the risk of a mentally disordered person doing serious harm to others. Since the introduction of the Act in 1959, little of substance relating to the compulsory admission and detention of non-offenders has changed. However, Part V has been considerably amended by the Children and Young Persons Act 1969, the Criminal Procedure (Insanity) Act 1964, the Criminal Justice Act 1967 and the Courts Act 1971. In addition, the Aarvold Report* recommended the introduction of a system whereby the responsible medical officer within three months of a "restricted" patient's admission, considers whether special care in assessment of the patient is necessary. An independent advisory board was established to assist the Home Secretary in making decisions involving any substantial relaxation of control over the patient. This system is already in operation in the Special Hospitals and the Butler Committee have recommended** that the advisory board should be reconstituted to enable it to help the Home Secretary in decisions relating to all "restricted" patients in Special Hospitals as well as to any "restricted" patients in a local hospital or regional security unit on whom an independent opinion would be helpful. The Home Secretary has accepted this recommendation in principle.

10.2 The Butler Committee were very conscious of the need to balance the safety of the public and the patient's interests. Their recommendations in this respect are discussed in paragraphs 10.4–10.24 below.

10.3 The Royal College's suggestion that there should be statutory provision for the examination and withholding of items transferred between a Special Hospital patient and another person is discussed in paragraphs 10.25–10.27. The general question of withholding correspondence is discussed in paragraphs 10.28–10.31.

Absconding patients

10.4 The Butler Committee considered*** section 40 (3), which limits the time during which absconding unrestricted detained patients can be returned to hospital—normally 28 days but, in the case of a psychopathic or subnormal patient over 21, six months.****

---

* Cmnd 5191.

** Cmnd 6244: paragraphs 4.21–4.25.

*** Ibid: paragraphs 14.13–14.16.

**** The Royal Commission's reason for recommending a longer period for the latter was that it was not possible for him to be readmitted once the original authority had lapsed. If age limits were to be removed, such a distinction would, in any case, no longer be necessary.

10.5 They felt that the reasons for allowing as little as 28 days for the return of a patient were no longer valid and that there would be merit in the introduction of a more flexible system. They also felt that the responsible medical officer should be free to decide whether or not continued detention was necessary since they could see little point in returning to hospital a patient who would not co-operate in treatment and who did not present a danger to the public. They therefore recommended that the responsible medical officer should be able to decide whether or not to require the return of an absconding patient at any time before the end of the current period of detention.

10.6 One difficulty about this recommendation is that, taken as it stands, it would mean that, in the case of a patient who absconded shortly before that date, the responsible medical officer would no longer have the benefit of the additional period of time which he has at present on the date of expiry in which to secure the patient's return. The provision in the Act is that, no matter when the patient absconds, the responsible medical officer always has the 28 days or 6 months referred to in paragraph 10.4 above in which to have him returned. It might therefore be preferable to retain an arrangement of this kind to cover the case of the patient who absconds shortly before his detention is due to end by providing a minimum period—say 6 months—during which he could be returned. Within these limits it seems right that the question of recall should be left to the discretion of the responsible medical officer but when he has no intention of seeking the patient's return he should be required formally to discharge him as soon as possible—perhaps within a week of his absconding.

Remand to hospital

10.7 The Committee felt that in relation to the trial of a mentally disordered person there were four situations in which the court should have the power to remand such a person to hospital before deciding his ultimate disposal*:

(i) where a medical report was required on a convicted defendant;

(ii) where the defendant required medical care during a custodial remand;

(iii) where a period in hospital was required to determine whether a hospital order was appropriate;

(iv) where the defendant was found under disability in relation to the trial.

10.8 The Committee point out that there is a precedent for remand to hospital in section 54 of the Mental Health (Scotland) Act 1960 although the primary purpose of that section is care for a mentally disordered person on remand. They go on to say that remand to prison may be unhelpful in view of the limited facilities of certain prisons for dealing with the generality of psychiatric cases. The present alternative method of obtaining a medical report on a defendant, where it is inappropriate to do this as an out-patient, is to grant bail with a condition of hospital residence; but this gives the hospital no power to detain the patient should he break the condition by discharging himself. The alternative method of remanding to prison and then transferring an offender under section 73 of the Mental Health Act has two disadvantages: the court itself cannot order such a transfer and the requirement for two doctors to state

* Cmnd 6244: paragraphs 12.1–12.14.

that the patient is suffering from either mental illness or severe subnormality anticipates the more considered diagnosis that it would be the purpose of a remand to hospital to obtain. Moreover, this procedure cannot be used for psychopathic or subnormal patients who present the greatest problem.

10.9 Where a defendant required medical care during a custodial remand, the Committee felt, the provision for remand to hospital when the defendant was awaiting trial or sentence would provide a simpler procedure than section 73.

10.10 They also felt that remand to hospital might be desirable where there was some doubt as to whether a defendant would benefit from a hospital order. They say

> "At present a hospital order may be made on medical recommendation but it may subsequently become clear that no treatment is possible; the patient may be unresponsive or disruptive, or he may even be found through continuous observation in hospital to have been feigning mental disorder at the time he was first examined. As the order cannot subsequently be replaced by a punitive sentence the hospital has no alternative in such a case but to discharge the patient and he is then beyond the reach of the court. This difficulty could in part be solved if the court had power to make what might be termed an "interim hospital order", committing the defendant to a specified hospital for a limited period of compulsory detention for diagnosis and assessment. At the latest at the expiry of the interim period, the court would again consider the case and would have discretion to confirm the order if the medical report so recommended, or, if the report indicated that a hospital order was inappropriate, to reconsider the matter and impose any other available disposal, including, where appropriate, a custodial sentence."*

The Committee considered that an offender subject to an interim order should remain subject to the jurisdiction of the court and should be liable to be returned to the court if he absconded.

10.11 In the case of a defendant found to be under disability in relation to trial, the Committee thought it ought to be possible to remand him to hospital if there was some indication that he would recover within a few months to the point of being able to stand trial. They thought that this measure might be used, for example, for dangerous offenders for whom psychiatric treatment as a condition of bail does not provide a sufficient measure of compulsion.

10.12 The Report goes on to recommend that one form of order should be made available for all four situations: it should enable the defendant to be remanded to a particular hospital (which might be a Special Hospital, regional security unit or local phsychiatric hospital) for an initial maximum of three months for the purpose of care, observation, assessment, treatment and report. Where the purpose of the order was to test the suitability of the substantive order or a preliminary to a possible finding of disability in relation to trial, the court should be empowered to extend the period a month at a time subject to an overall maximum of six months.

10.13 The Committee did not intend the defendant to be remanded to hospital if bail could be given nor did they wish him to remain in hospital any longer

* Cmnd 6244: paragraph 12.5.

than was necessary to achieve the object of the remand. They concluded that medical evidence was necessary before a defendant could be remanded to hospital. This could be given orally by any doctor in relation to remand for medical reports or for care or remand on disability proceedings but, in the case of interim hospital orders, written or oral evidence should be given by two medical practitioners, one of them being "approved" under section 28 of the Mental Health Act and normally being the receiving doctor. At least one should give evidence orally if a section 65 order were contemplated. The Committee considered that it should not be necessary to recall the defendant to court at the end of his remand to hospital if the court were to be advised to confirm an interim order or if a hospital order were to be recommended in a case of disability. Section 76(2) of the Mental Health Act is cited as a precedent: this section provides that under certain circumstances the court may make a hospital order for a patient who has been transferred to a hospital while in custody awaiting trial or sentence without bringing him before the court again.

10.14 It is felt that these recommendations represent a useful addition to the flexibility of criminal courts and their ability to dispose of each case in the most appropriate way. There might also be certain benefits for the hospitals. In the first place, the Committee thought that the observation of patients on remand and preparation of reports in a hospital setting rather in the variable conditions and facilities of a Prison Department establishment would help to reduce the likelihood of an incorrect diagnosis being made and the consequent possibility of what is later discovered to be an inappropriate disposal by the court. At present, an offender who is made the subject of a hospital order after evidence of mental disorder and who is subsequently found to be unsuitable for hospital treatment or not to need it, must either be discharged or kept in hospital for purely custodial reasons which is generally considered to be both wrong in principle and a misuse of hospital resources. Conversely, of course, the risk that a defendant who is suffering from an undiagnosed mental disorder would be committed on conviction to a prison environment, where suitable treatment for his disorder may not be available, should be reduced. It is not clear, however, that it would be possible, as the Butler Committee envisaged, to create just one form of order for the different situations in which remand to hospital may be appropriate. The remands would serve different purposes and the Committee recommended varying maximum remand periods and varying requirements as to the medical evidence on which the order would have to be based. Moreover, certain of the recommendations, for example, those relating to medical reports and unfitness for trial, need to be examined, not only within the context of this review but also in relation to criminal procedure generally.

10.15 As far as the hospitals are concerned it seems clear that the need in general to provide secure accommodation for defendants remanded in custody will place serious limitations on the extent to which the court will be able to use any powers to remand direct to hospital. The Committee thought that, while some defendants would need the security of regional security units (or even Special Hospitals where appropriate) others could be accommodated in local hospitals. The Committee do not appear to have thought that this should place any additional responsibility to provide secure accommodation on these hospitals, on the basis that the courts would in making their decisions take into account the level of security afforded by the various hospitals to which it would be possible to remand a defendant. In fact it seems likely that the regional security units would have the major role to play in accepting remanded defendants and since it is only planned at this stage to provide a thousand places it is unlikely that their contribution will be very great. It is also doubtful whether the courts could see advantage in remanding a defendant who needs the security of only a local hospital to the custody of that hospital rather than requiring his residence there as a condition of bail. In this connection the Butler Committee's view that remands to hospital should not be regarded as an alternative to observation or treatment on bail is relevant; so too is the Government's Bail Bill (now before Parliament) which provides that there should be a statutory presumption in favour of bail, to a person whose case is adjourned after conviction but before sentence, for the purpose of enabling enquiries or a report to be made.

10.16 Another safeguard which might be introduced into the procedure is indicated by the Committee's view that, in the case of remand to hospital for observation or report, there should be a prior assurance from the hospital to which a court is minded to remand the defendant that a place is available and, in the case of interim hospital orders, that one of the two doctors whose medical recommendations are necessary before an order can be made should be the consultant responsible for the patient in the receiving hospital. It would be necessary to ensure that, in all cases, the consultant in question was involved in the decision to remand him to hospital.

Section 65

10.17 The Butler Committee recommended* that section 65(1) should be more precisely worded in order to indicate its essential purpose, namely to protect the public from serious harm. At present the section permits a Crown Court to make a restriction order if "it appears to the Court, having regard to the nature of the offence, the antecedents of the offender and the risk of his committing further offences if set at large, that it is necessary for the protection of the public so to do". The Committee considered that, although there has been a decline over recent years in the number of cases in which the section has been applied after the commission of less serious offences, the fact that the wording of the section did not indicate the seriousness of the offences from which the public is intended to be protected meant that some courts had inappropriately imposed restrictions: for example, on a petty recidivist because of the virtual certainty that he would persist in similar offences in future.

10.18 Another recommendation is that, because of the difficulty of predicting future behaviour, the provisions for a court to make a restriction order of limited duration should be removed from the statute.** In practice this could be achieved by amending section 65 so that no reference is made either to specified periods of time or to its being without limit of time. The Court would thus simply have to refer to "restriction under section 65" in making an order. At present if a restriction is without limit of time the defendant may

* Cmnd 6244: paragraph 14.24.
** Ibid: paragraph 14.25.

see it as equivalent to a "life" sentence and refuse to co-operate in treatment; or, if a certain number of years is specified, it may be misinterpreted by the patient, the press and the public as equivalent to a penal sentence. These difficulties would not arise if the recommendation were accepted. On the other hand, those defendants for whom the Courts now feel a limited restriction to be appropriate would have to be subject to the indeterminacy of a restriction without limit of time.

10.19 Together with this, the Committee also recommended* that to ensure that a "restricted" patient is not detained longer than necessary, an annual report on him should be submitted to the Home Secretary by the responsible medical officer.

10.20 All three of these recommendations seem acceptable and it might be a helpful clarification if the submission of annual reports were made a statutory requirement.

10.21 The Committee also recommended that there should be a statutory requirement for the consent of the doctor to accepting a patient subject to a section 65 restriction order to be required before such an order is made by the Court.** The fact that a restriction order requires the Home Secretary to give his consent to the discharge, transfer or leave of the patient makes some doctors feel unduly restrained in providing treatment and not free to make their own decisions in these crucial areas. Although this is understandable, the Court must clearly be able to make such arrangements as it considers necessary for the control of dangerous offenders. It also seems likely that some doctors do not understand the effect and purpose of restriction orders. Much could be done to increase the co-operation of receiving doctors by consulting them beforehand about suggestions that restrictions should be imposed. It is not thought that this should be made a statutory requirement but rather that there is scope for administrative action to encourage such co-operation.

Admission by Order of the Home Secretary to a "Place of Safety"

10.22 The Butler Committee proposed that there should be provision for the Home Secretary to authorise the emergency admission for a period of up to 72 hours to a "place of safety" of a conditionally discharged "restricted" patient if advised that, in the opinion of the patient's supervising officer, recall to hospital is justified by his behaviour but a hospital place cannot immediately be obtained.*** The suggestion is that the "place of safety" should be a regional security unit, but that, until such units are in being, it should be the hospital of a local remand prison or remand centre. The reasoning behind this suggestion seems to be that, although immediate admission to hospital may be essential in the supervising officer's view, recall can in practice prove difficult to arrange since the consent of the consultant to accept the patient is necessary.

---

* Cmnd 6244: paragraph 14.25.
** Ibid: paragraph 14.22.
*** Ibid: paragraphs 14.28–14.32.

10.23 The recommendation ties in with others relating to the discharge of "restricted" patients, one of which is that the responsible medical officer and the Home Office should agree before discharge on the circumstances in which the patient could be accepted on recall.* If this were adopted there should be less dispute about the appropriateness of recall although the practical difficulties mentioned above might remain. However, there is doubt about whether it would be possible to draw up an agreed set of circumstances justifying recall which was neither too specific nor too general.

10.24 It is not thought appropriate that, to meet a situation in which recall is resisted by the consultant or is difficult to arrange for other reasons, the provisions in the Act to admit patients under emergency procedures for up to 72 hours should be extended further in the way the Committee recommend. It seems unrealistic to assume that a responsible medical officer who knew the circumstances of a discharged "restricted" patient who had been under his care would change his mind about the desirability of recall within a 72-hour period and whether, in any case, 72 hours would be long enough if the responsible medical officer were absent for any reason. In addition, it is arguable whether it is right to use (even in the interim period) a penal institution as a "place of safety" without any new offence having been committed. The Committee recommended that, after this interim period, the regional security unit should be used but, being a hospital, such a unit would satisfy the conditions as to recall laid down in section 66 (b). It seems that what the Butler Committee may have intended is that, although they recommend a statutory requirement that the receiving doctor give his consent to admission of a restricted patient,** in the case of recall to a "place of safety" for the limited period suggested, such consent should not be required. This would be to use the hospital purely as a place of detention until a bed could be found.

10.25 It might be thought preferable that supervising officers and hospital staff should keep in closer touch with each other and try to agree on what is practicable.

Withholding of items in the interests of security

10.26 The Royal College of Psychiatrists have suggested that the Act should make specific provision to give the staff in Special Hospitals the right to inspect and withhold any item transferred between a patient and any other person. Certainly it is necessary in view of the types of patient for whom they are responsible for Special Hospital staff to take precautions to ensure that patients do not acquire weapons or other implements which may be used for self-mutilation, attacks on other people or escape attempts.

10.27 But the problem is not confined to Special Hospitals. There are patients in local hospitals, both detained and informal, who might be a danger to themselves or others if they acquired weapons. Indeed, perhaps the greatest staff anxiety relates to informal patients, now that the House of Lords ruling has made it clear that the control of detained patients is carried out in pursuance of the Act and therefore covered by section 141 (see Chapter 9 above).

---

* Cmnd 6244: paragraph 14.30.
** Ibid: paragraph 4.22.

10.28 However, the DHSS legal advisers are of the opinion that staff have the authority at common law and by virtue of section 3 (1) of the Criminal Law Act 1967, to take reasonable measures to prevent a patient from keeping in his possession articles of potential danger such as matches, weapons, alcohol, tools, explosives, etc. This opinion has been stated in official guidance in circular HC(76)11* and should reassure staff about their right to take action of this sort without the need for supporting specific legislation.

WITHOLDING OF CORRESPONDENCE

10.29 The Royal Commission recommended that "there should be no censorship of outgoing letters from patients (whether subject to detention or not) except at the request of individual addressees who ask for letters addressed to themselves to be scrutinised or witheld because they find them distressing. The hospital authority should have authority to withhold from patients any incoming letters which it would harm them to receive but this power should be sparingly used . . . . . whenever a letter is witheld from a patient it should be returned to the writer."**
Under section 36 (applied to informal patients by section 134(1)), postal packets may be witheld on the authority of the responsible medical officer in the circumstances recommended by the Royal Commission but also "if it appears to that officer that the package would be unreasonably offensive to the addressee or is defamatory of other persons (other than persons on the staff of the hospital) or would be likely to prejudice the interests of the patient." Mail addressed to certain people or groups of people identified in the section is excluded in these provisions and it is intended that the European Committee on Human Rights and Community Health Councils should be added to the list.

10.30 The MIND Report*** discusses the provisions in the Act and makes a number of different criticisms:

(i) that censorship discourages a form of communication that may be of therapeutic value;

(ii) that censorship is a form of restraint of freedom of speech which should be used with great care and only for well defined reasons;

(iii) that the statutory provisions may be applied in practice to all patients in a hospital including informal patients (under section 134) because of the needs of a few;

(iv) that the responsible medical officer is required to make a non-medical judgement which he is not qualified to make;

(v) that he is not accountable for his decisions; and

(vi) that patients are not told whether or not their mail is to be censored.

(This use of the term "censorship" is misleading as the Act makes no provision for deleting passages of a letter.)

---

* Management of Violent or Potentially Violent Hospital Patients.
** Cmnd 169: paragraph 299.
*** A Human Condition: Vol I pages 111–114.

10.31 Section 36 was certainly drafted at a time when conditions in psychiatric hospitals were very different from those of the present day. The examination of outgoing mail is rarely practised in local hospitals nowadays because of the number of informal patients who are able to move in and out and it is certainly often possible for even a detained patient to avoid the responsible medical officer's scrutiny of his mail, simply by having it posted by another patient. One situation in which it may be desirable to prevent a letter from reaching its intended destination is when a patient convicted of an offence of violence writes to his victim or the victim's relatives. Even if such a letter is an expression of regret, the recipient may find it extremely distressing and may feel justified in protesting strongly at the fact that the letter was not stopped. On the other hand, a doctor can only base the decision to withhold such a letter on his own subjective judgement which may inaccurately predict the addressee's reaction. A tendency to write offensive letters is not necessarily connected, moreover, with dangerousness or violence and it is just as likely that such letters will be sent from local hospitals as from Special Hospitals. Although inspection of mail is undoubtedly easier in conditions of security, to retain the power of inspection only for patients in such conditions would be to make an unjustifiable distinction between these patients and patients in other hospital units.

10.32 The Department's attention has not been drawn to any particular problems which have arisen in practice in relation to withholding mail and it is therefore suggested that the power of inspection should be retained. However, in order to prevent the kind of situation which MIND describe in which patients believe that all their mail is censored, it is suggested that a statutory requirement be introduced that a patient must be told if his mail is examined or witheld so that, failing this, he may rest assured that his letters are not being interfered with.

CHAPTER 11. SUMMARY AND CONCLUSIONS TO PART II

11.1 Several developments aimed at providing additional protection for patients have been introduced since the 1959 Act. (Paras 8.1–8.2).

11.2 Mental Health Review Tribunals could not be replaced by mental welfare commissions since their functions are rather different. (Para 8.4).

11.3 It would not be practicable to introduce a system of hearings within 5–10 days after admission but some form of early and periodic automatic review for "unrestricted" patients might be introduced. It is suggested that, if annual reports are to be made to the Home Secretary on all "restricted" patients, the present intervals at which the Home Secretary may refer cases to Tribunals may not require to be changed. However, an automatic review for such patients after, say, 4 or 5 years might be introduced. At least a doubling of the present workload of Tribunals should be possible. Comments are invited in particular from Mental Health Review Tribunal Chairmen and members on the feasibility of increasing their workload and by how much it would be possible to do this. (Paras 8.5–8.11).

11.4 Tribunals are at present unduly restricted by being able to choose only between ordering the discharge of a patient and leaving him subject to detention. A number of proposals for widening their powers are discussed. It is thought that they might be given power to direct delayed discharge, but only to recommend transfer, trial leave and conditional discharges. Such recommendations would be expected to carry considerable weight. (Paras 8.12–8.17).

11.5 The suggestion that an application should be withdrawn only with the Tribunal's permission and that it should not prevent another application from being made within the period, is endorsed. (Para 8.18).

11.6 The use of forensic psychiatrists as medical members of Tribunals and the addition of a social work member to a Tribunal might be useful. (Para 8.19).

11.7 The issue of consent to treatment requires to be clarified. The Butler suggestion that only treatment intended to prevent violence, save life, or prevent deterioration, should be carried out without consent, is thought to be acceptable, as is the suggestion that a second opinion should be sought when a form of treatment is proposed which is irreversible or hazardous. There are certain disadvantages in requiring that this second opinion should be a medical one but there would also be difficulty in enabling the second opinion to be given by a member of another profession. The MIND proposal for a Committee on the Rights and Responsibilities of Staff and Residents of Psychiatric Hospitals is thought to be too cumbersome, but there might be a case for multi-professional panels at hospital, area or regional levels whose purpose would be to provide a second opinion where the doctor proposes a form of treatment which is irreversible, hazardous or not fully established. (Paras 8.20–8.27).

11.8 The question of treatment for a patient detained for observation is discussed. It is felt that only treatment designed to prevent him from being violent or to save his life should be given without his consent to a patient detained under section 25. If anything further is thought to be required, a section 26 order should be sought. (Paras 8.28–8.29).

11.9 The relevance of the earlier discussion to informal patients is discussed and it is suggested that, in any proposal to give irreversible or hazardous treatment to an informal patient, the proposed panel might be asked to give a second opinion, even if the patient were able to give and had given an informed consent. (Paras 8.30–8.31).

11.10 Ways of implementing these proposals are discussed and particularly the means of distinguishing between "acceptable" forms of treatment and those for which a second opinion is required. On balance it is thought that the most satisfactory way of doing this would be to issue guidance stating general principles and to rely upon the good judgement and goodwill of staff and patients in co-operating in arrangements for treatment within that wide framework. (Paras 8.32–8.37).

11.11 The suggestion that mental welfare commissions should be introduced is discussed and the various drawbacks pointed out. (Paras 8.38–8.42).

11.12 The possibility of extending the Butler Committee recommendation that there should be statutory provision for the appointment of patients' friends to all patients is discussed and reference made to the difficulties of doing so. (Para 8.43).

11.13 The MIND suggestion of an advocacy system is considered and it is suggested that this would be too complicated and expensive. (Paras 8.44–8.47).

11.14 It is suggested that, if there is a need for such additional protection for the mentally disordered, patients' advisers might be appointed to advise the mentally disordered of their rights and of the formal complaint procedures. Such advisers might be employed on behalf of Community Health Councils, although there would be disadvantages in this, or voluntary organisations might be given Government assistance to enable them to provide this service. Views are invited on whether such a development is thought to be feasible, in which case the DHSS will consider funding an experiment. (Paras 8.48–8.49).

11.15 The extent of the protection afforded by section 141 is not entirely clear and Treasury Counsel's opinion has been sought. The areas of doubt relate to treatment of detained patients, treatment of informal patients and control of informal patients. The various criticisms of the protection are discussed and the conclusion drawn is that something similar is required but that, in its present form, it is too sweeping. A number of possibilities are discussed and those preferred are:

(*a*) that administrative action should be taken in the form of guidance on such matters as control and consent to treatment;

(*b*) that criminal actions including those for common assault should be removed from the scope of section 141 and made subject to scrutiny by the Director of Public Prosecutions;

(*c*) that the word "substantial" should be removed and the word "reasonable" substituted. (Paras 9.1–9.14).

11.16 The Butler recommendation that the decision whether or not to recall an absconding patient should be left to the discretion of the responsible medical officer is thought to be acceptable, with the proviso that it might be preferable if the power to recall did not expire until after a period of 6 months in case the patient had absconded shortly before the end of his period of detention. The responsible medical officer might also be required to make a decision within a specified period—say a week—as to whether or not to recall the patient and, if not, to discharge him. (Paras 10.4–10.6).

11.17 The Butler recommendations on remand to hospital are discussed and thought to be generally acceptable although some require to be examined in the context of criminal procedures generally. If the difficulties can be overcome and remand to hospital introduced, it will be necessary to ensure that the consultant responsible for the patient in the receiving hospital is in each case involved beforehand in the decision to remand a defendant to hospital. Comments are invited on the practicability of the recommendations and whether this safeguard should be given statutory effect. (Paras 10.7–10.16).

11.18 Three Butler recommendations for amending section 65 are discussed. The recommendation that its essential purpose, namely to protect the public from serious harm, should be made clear is thought to be acceptable as is the recommendation that restriction should in all cases be without limit of time. As a safeguard it is suggested that the requirement on the responsible medical officer to submit an annual report to the Home Secretary should be made statutory. The recommendation that the consent of the receiving consultant should be obtained before a restriction order is made is felt to be a matter for administrative action rather than legislation. (Paras 10.17–10.21).

11.19 It is argued that the Butler recommendation that the Home Secretary should be able to recall a conditionally discharged "restricted" patient to a "place of safety" for 72 hours should not be accepted. Instead it is suggested that supervising officers and hospital staff should keep in close touch with each other and try to agree on what is practicable. (Paras 10.22–10.25)

11.20 A suggestion that the staff of the Special Hospitals should have legislative power to inspect and withhold any item passed between a patient and another person is discussed. Existing powers are considered adequate. (Paras 10.26–10.28).

11.21 MIND's criticisms of the power in section 36, extended by section 134 to apply to informal patients, which enables the responsible medical officer to examine and withhold postal packets to or from patients are discussed. It is pointed out that, outside the Special Hospitals, the power to inspect outgoing mail is little used in practice, but it is argued that the authority for doing so if necessary should not be removed. Instead, as a safeguard to patients, it is suggested that there should be a statutory requirement that a patient be informed if his correspondence is being examined. (Paras 10.29–10.32).

APPENDIX I

Mental Health Act 1959

Definition and Classification of Mental Disorder

Section 4 of the Mental Health Act 1959 reads as follows:

1. In this Act "mental disorder" means mental illness, arrested or incomplete development of mind, psychopathic disorder, and any other disorder or disability of mind; and "mentally disordered" shall be construed accordingly.

2. In this Act "severe subnormality" means a state of arrested or incomplete development of mind which includes subnormality of intelligence and is of such a nature or degree that the patient is incapable of living an independent life or of guarding himself against serious exploitation, or will be so incapable when of an age to do so.

3. In this Act "subnormality" means a state of arrested or incomplete development of mind (not amounting to severe subnormality) which includes subnormality of intelligence and is of a nature or degree which requires or is susceptible to medical treatment or other special care or training of the patient.

4. In this Act "psychopathic disorder" means a persistent disorder or disability of mind (whether or not including subnormality of intelligence) which results in abnormally aggressive or seriously irresponsible conduct on the part of the patient and requires or is susceptible to medical treatment.

5. Nothing in this section shall be construed as implying that a person may be dealt with under this Act as suffering from mental disorder, or from any form of mental disorder described in this section, by reason only of promiscuity or other immoral conduct.

An example of how a "closed" definition of mental disorder might be achieved

The example set out below is not intended as an attempt at drafting for amending legislation but simply as an indication of the way in which the aim of tightening up on the definitions used in the Act might be tackled.

1. *Mental disorder* means (*a*) mental illness or (*b*) severe subnormality or (*c*) severe personality disorder or (*d*) severe behavioural reaction.

   (*a*) *Mental illness* means an illness having one or more of the following characteristics

   (i) More than temporary impairment of intellectual functions shown by a failure of memory, orientation, comprehension and learning capacity.

   (ii) More than temporary alteration of mood of such degree as to give rise to the patient having a delusional appraisal of his situation, his past or his future, or that of others or to the lack of any appraisal.

   (iii) Delusional beliefs, persecutory, jealous or grandiose.

   (iv) Abnormal perceptions associated with delusional misinterpretation of events.

   (v) Thinking so disordered as to prevent the patient making a reasonable appraisal of his situation or having reasonable communication with others.

   The mental illness should be of a nature or degree which warrants the detention of the patient in the interest of his health or safety or for the protection of others.

   (*b*) *Severe mental subnormality* means a state of arrested or incomplete development of mind which includes subnormality of intelligence and is of such a nature or degree that the patient is incapable of living an independent life or of guarding himself against serious exploitation, or will be so incapable when of an age to do so.

   (*c*) *Severe personality disorder* means a persistent abnormality of mind of such a kind and degree as seriously to affect the person's life or adjustment to society, and which is so marked as to render him a serious risk to himself or to others.

   (*d*) *Severe behaviour reaction* means a behavioural or mental reaction of the personality to circumstances which is so marked as to render the person a serious risk to himself or to others.

2. Some further explanation of the intention and scope of the above categories may be of help in understanding why these particular sub-categories are used:

   (*a*) The suggested definition of "mental illness" is based on the definition of "severe mental illness" proposed by the Butler

Committee in connection with the recommendation for a new statutory test for the special verdict in place of the M'Naghten Rules. Although the Committee suggested the definition in a much more specialised legal context than that considered in this Document it does set out the basic characteristics of mental illness and these are obviously of general relevance. The definition proposed by the Committee has been amended to make it more appropriate to the needs of the Mental Health Act by the omission of "severe" and by the amendment of the temporal description in categories i and ii from "lasting" to "more than temporary". These changes, together with the added criterion that the illness should be judged to be of a nature or degree which warrants detention in the interests of his own safety or the protection of others, are thought to be sufficient to distinguish the definition from that proposed in connection with the special verdict. The aim is that mental illness should be closely defined in terms which are readily understood by clinicians and which would enable close monitoring and debate on individual decisions in contrast to the present arrangement whereby "mental illness" is not defined.

(*b*) This definition is the same as that for severe subnormality in the present Act. The separate category of "subnormality" is omitted since the criteria for detention are other than subnormality of intelligence *per se* and it is felt that any person who is mentally handicapped and in need of detention would come under one of the other sub-categories. (See Appendix III).

(*c*) This uses the WHO definition of personality disorder as a basis—see paragraph 1.21.

Removal of the Mentally Handicapped from the jurisdiction of the Mental Health Act

1. This Appendix discusses some of the arguments for and against the removal of mental handicap from the jurisdiction of the Mental Health Act 1959. Views would be welcomed on this.

2. The major arguments for removal of mental handicap from the scope of the Act appear to be:

(*a*) that inclusion in the Act has the effect of equating mental subnormality (or mental handicap as it is now termed) with other forms of mental incapacity, and of giving the impression that it is a form of psychiatric disorder;

(*b*) that the factors which warrant the detention of some mentally handicapped people in hospital are more usually due to added psychiatric or behaviour disorder than to intellectual retardation and diminished social competence.

3. Against these points one must weigh the view that the central purpose of the Act's compulsory powers of detention in hospital is to provide treatment (a term which includes care) where this is essential either in a person's own interests or for the protection of others. The need arises because the various forms of mental disorder can affect an individual's reason and judgement and his appreciation of the effect of his behaviour on himself and others. The disorder may be such as to render him unable to care for himself or live an independent life or to behave in such an irresponsible way as to endanger others. It would be difficult to deny that mental handicap cannot, in any circumstances, have such an effect.

4. The level of intelligence of the severely handicapped adult may make him heavily dependent on others but his physical size and strength may pose special problems in caring for him and controlling his behaviour. In the vast majority of cases necessary care is provided without recourse to compulsory powers but where such a person is being neglected or exploited or where his behaviour is such that it cannot be sufficiently controlled by those looking after him it may be necessary to ensure that proper care is given.

5. The vast majority of those who fall within the Mental Health Act definition of subnormality (that is those who are mildly rather than severely handicapped) are able with varying degrees of advice and support to establish themselves in adult life with few problems. But a lack of understanding or lack of social skills may lead someone who is mentally handicapped (or cause him to allow himself to be led) into behaviour which endangers or is offensive to others, or may make him vulnerable to exploitation. It seems possible that many of these situations can be ascribed to supervening mental illness or personality disorder. If such an individual's behaviour brings him in conflict with the law however, it is for consideration whether it is right to regard him as wholly responsible. The proportion of subnormal patients detained as a result of orders made by the Courts is, in practice, higher than that of the

mentally ill. The Courts not infrequently choose a hospital rather than a penal disposal, partly for humane considerations but also because they hope this will afford the offender the help, advice and training he needs to establish himself in society. It is arguable whether it would be in the best interests of the mentally handicapped to take away this facility.

6. The point that mental handicap is not a medical condition, in the sense of being susceptible to what is normally regarded as medical treatment, is one which perhaps needs greater recognition in the Act. The Act defines medical treatment as including nursing and also including care and training under medical supervision; and it is these aspects which may need greater emphasis. The words of the Butler Committee in this context are relevant to the mentally handicapped offender:

> "It is not sufficiently recognised, or always remembered, that the Act defines medical treatment as including not only nursing but also care and training under medical supervision (section 147(1)). Subnormality is often not treatable except in this limited sense, but no one would suggest that it should, on that account, be excluded from the Act or from the hospitals." (Para 5.2.1, page 85).

7. If mental subnormality were to be removed from the Act, the present safeguards, not only for the public but also for the mentally handicapped themselves, could not be allowed to disappear and great care would be needed to ensure that these were provided in some other form. This could well be a complex exercise and this document has not attempted to pursue the alternative safeguards which would be required. It would be useful to know, however, whether there is any widespread view that the mentally handicapped should be removed from the jurisdiction of the Act and, if so, what alternative safeguards should be provided.

8. There would also be a need to ensure that powers to provide services and facilities for the mentally handicapped which are incorporated in other legislation, but which depend upon their inclusion within the definition of mental disorder in the Mental Health Act, were not lost and that in consequence no rights or access to services were also lost. The points made in this paragraph and paragraph 7 above come up against a difficulty that it might not be possible to effect all the changes in one Parliamentary Bill and it is unlikely that the legislative programme would be such as to enable there to be two separate Bills in one year.

9. But whether or not there emerges a clear view for or against the removal of mental subnormality from mental health legislation, comments would be welcome on the necessity for and adequacy of the present definitions (bearing in mind that mental illness is not defined in the present Act) and in particular on the need separately to define severe subnormality.

Mental illness and mental handicap hospitals and teaching hospitals in England and Wales

Regions	Admission under section 29 M H Act as a percentage of all admissions under sections 25, 26 and 29 combined									
	1964	1965	1966	1967	1968	1969	1970	1971	1972	1973
England and Wales	62·9	60·5	56·5	51·4	54·2	56·6	58·4	61·3	62·0	62·5
Newcastle	68·2	68·4	72·5	63·3	70·7	72·3	74·5	75·6	76·5	78·0
Leeds	67·6	67·7	69·0	70·2	72·7	76·9	79·8	78·9	79·6	78·3
Sheffield	68·6	62·6	55·3	41·8	48·1	53·5	55·3	62·1	62·4	66·3
East Anglia	73·6	79·6	71·8	70·0	73·1	79·0	79·9	78·9	79·4	78·8
North West Metropolitan	63·9	62·5	58·9	55·5	57·6	58·8	58·8	62·2	56·6	50·6
North East ,,	70·3	68·4	69·3	62·5	63·1	68·9	72·7	73·3	72·4	74·0
South East ,,	69·1	68·5	63·6	57·4	56·7	56·9	58·9	59·2	64·1	61·4
South West ,,	62·9	56·7	55·5	55·2	55·4	55·2	55·2	59·7	61·6	61·1
Oxford	34·3	36·7	35·6	28·1	29·1	32·6	35·0	42·8	41·5	41·7
South Western	58·1	57·1	46·9	46·1	51·2	51·3	52·4	55·4	57·3	57·7
Birmingham	52·8	51·6	45·6	41·1	39·1	44·5	48·8	52·2	52·7	49·9
Manchester	44·8	41·6	34·0	32·5	37·7	43·5	46·4	49·4	52·0	58·2
Liverpool	62·7	54·0	51·6	39·2	41·8	37·5	37·1	43·6	35·3	34·8
Wessex	66·1	63·4	60·9	48·1	55·9	51·9	55·4	55·2	58·6	66·6
Wales	88·3	87·9	81·9	79·8	81·5	81·2	82·8	84·4	86·7	84·2

APPENDIX V

Guardianship

		Mentally Ill	Mentally Handicapped	Total
A. ENGLAND				
at 31 December	1960	1	1088	1089
	1961	13	705	718
	1962	21	645	666
	1963	22	492	514
	1964	20	416	436
	1965	20	362	382
	1966	17	302	319
	1967	16	285	301
	1968	14	260	274
	1969	18	226	244
	1970	20	204	224
at 31 March	1972*			218
	1973	23	158	181
	1974	24	125	149
B. WALES				
at 31 December	1960	–	44	44
	1961	1	13	14
	1962	–	12	12
	1963	–	9	9
	1964	–	9	9
	1965	–	6	6
	1966	1	6	7
	1967	1	7	8
	1968	1	9	10
	1969	2	7	9
	1970	2	3	4
at 31 March	1972	1	4	5
	1973	1	7	8
	1974	1	9	10

* No analysis available.

Scottish Mental Welfare Commission
Mental Health (Scotland) Act 1960

Section 4

1. It shall be the duty of the Mental Welfare Commission generally to exercise protective functions in respect of persons who may, by reason of mental disorder, be incapable of adequately protecting their persons or their interests, and, where those persons are liable to be detained in hospital or subject to guardianship under the following provisions of this Act, their functions as aforesaid shall include, in appropriate cases, the discharge of such patients in accordance with the said provisions.

2. In the exercise of their functions as aforesaid it shall be the duty of the Mental Welfare Commission—

(*a*) to make enquiry into any case where it appears to them that there may be ill treatment, deficiency in care or treatment, or improper detention of any person who may be suffering from mental disorder, or where the property of any such person may, by reason of his mental disorder, be exposed to loss or damage;

(*b*) to visit regularly, and as often as they may think appropriate, patients who are liable to be detained in hospital or who are subject to guardianship, and on any such visit to afford an opportunity, on request, for private interview to any such patient as aforesaid or, where the patient is in a hospital, to any other patient in that hospital;

(*c*) to bring to the attention of any board of management* or to any local authority the facts of any case in which in the opinion of the Mental Welfare Commission it is desirable for the board of management or the local authority to exercise any of the functions of that board or of that authority to secure the welfare of any patient suffering from mental disorder by—

(i) preventing his ill treatment;

(ii) remedying any deficiency in his care or treatment;

(iii) terminating his improper detention; or

(iv) preventing or redressing lawful damage to his property.

---

* For an NHS hospital this now means the health board.

Printed in England for Her Majesty's Stationery Office by Bemrose & Sons Ltd., Derby
Dd. 507274 K32 7/76

Scottish Mental Welfare Commission Mental Health (Scotland) Act 1960

Section 4

1. It shall be the duty of the Mental Welfare Commission generally to exercise protective functions in respect of persons who may by reason of mental disorder be incapable of adequately protecting their persons or their interests, and where those persons are liable to be detained in hospital or subject to guardianship under the following provisions of this Act, their functions as aforesaid shall include, in appropriate cases, the discharge of such patients in accordance with the said provisions.

2. In the exercise of their functions [illegible] it shall be the duty of the Mental Welfare Commission:

(a) to make enquiry into any case where it appears to them that there may be ill-treatment, deficiency in care or treatment, or improper detention of any person who may be suffering from mental disorder, or where the property of any such person may, by reason of his mental disorder, be exposed to loss or damage;

(b) to visit regularly, and as often as they may think appropriate, patients who are liable to be detained in hospital [illegible] or subject to guardianship, and on any such visit to afford an opportunity, on request, for private interview to any such patient [illegible] or any patient receiving treatment in a hospital [illegible] or any other part of the hospital;

(c) to bring to the attention of the board of management [illegible] or local authority the facts of any case in which in the opinion of the Mental Welfare Commission it is desirable for the board [illegible] or the local authority to exercise any of their functions [illegible] in order to secure the welfare of any patient suffering from mental disorder by:

(i) preventing his ill-treatment;

(ii) remedying any deficiency in his care or treatment;

(iii) terminating his improper detention; or

(iv) preventing or redressing loss or damage to his property.